Coming In

Coming In

✦

A Cowhand's Perspective

Ron Jordan
Author of Considerations—Emails
From the Heart

iUniverse, Inc.
New York Lincoln Shanghai

Coming In
A Cowhand's Perspective

iUniverse books may be ordered through booksellers or by contacting:

iUniverse
2021 Pine Lake Road, Suite 100
Lincoln, NE 68512
www.iuniverse.com
1-800-Authors (1-800-288-4677)

ISBN-13: 978-0-595-42486-3 (pbk)
ISBN-13: 978-0-595-86820-9 (ebk)
ISBN-10: 0-595-42486-4 (pbk)
ISBN-10: 0-595-86820-7 (ebk)

Printed in the United States of America

For Buck and Eva Jeanne Holmes …

Who placed their *trust* in me when others were in doubt,

Who gave me the *opportunity* to write,

And who gave me a *home* when I was without.

Thank you!

Contents

Preface

There are things I could wish for but know that I'll never obtain. Thirty-eight years ago I dreamt of wide-open skies, rolling plains and searching as far as I could possibly see. I arrived in Wyoming as a young man filled with hope and ambition ... I was not disappointed in what I found. Thirty-eight years is a long time ago and a lot has happened in that intervening time. I have since climbed the mountains, traversed the deserts, drank from the glacial streams and bedded within the bosom of the forest. More recently my life has been here, upon the rolling plains of southeastern Wyoming. My *spirit* still flies with the hawk, always searching and discovering what was previously missed in my first flights.

This book is an attempt to define *insanity* in a sometimes sane world. The loneliness, dejection, and sometimes lack of appreciation coupled with hard work could make any sane person absolutely crazy if they weren't a bit on the insanity side to begin with. I know that I will offend some folks both in the language that I use and the subject matter within these pages, but I make no apologies for either. The fact remains that this is the ranch hand's *life* as we have come to know it and to live it here in this portion of the prairie. I cannot apologize for *reality*.

Terminology is somewhat difficult. I use words interchangeably at times—ranch hand, cowpoke, cowboy, and cowhand for example. They all mean the same and that is just *plain hard work*. When *Cheyenne Frontier Days* rolls around towards the end of every July everyone thinks of themselves as cowboys and cowgirls and many even attempt to dress the part with their recently purchased cowboy hat. At the conclusion of *Cheyenne Frontier Days* all the *cowboys* and *cowgirls* disappear for another year except those still getting the work done out here on the ranches, day after day, every day of the year—ranchers and ranch hands alike.

Coming In is about the end of the work day when you're bone-tired and dragging ass. Every ounce of energy is depleted and you're praying that there's at least one more *cold one* still left in the refrigerator. Off with the boots, plop down on that old bunkhouse sofa, turn on the boob tube, and sip some suds, all the while wondering how in the hell you ever made it through the day. And then it comes to you in two words that you live by everyday ... *Cowboy Up*!

Part One—Hanging On

"Damn it Jim, I thought you said he could ride a horse!"

The two men glanced at the dust-covered form lying on the ground a hundred yards in the distance.

"He said he could, Bill."

"Well, it appears to me the only thing he's riding is the ground right now!"

Both of them watched as the other man's horse continued bucking at its non-existent rider and heading the opposite direction.

"That's just great—now we'll have to catch the damn horse and probably fix a broken-up kid as well. What the hell made you think the kid could ride a horse, Jim?"

"It was in his resume, Bill. It said he was good at riding horses and working with cattle."

"His resume! Are you out of your damn mind, Jim? You don't hire a man just because he says he can do something and it's on a piece of paper. Resume my ass! Now I got a horse heading for the high country and a kid as close to the earth as you can get, and you're talking about somebody's qualifications you read on a piece of paper. What the hell is this world coming to?"

"It's the modern times I reckon," Jim said.

The distant form slowly began to move as both men walked towards the kid's direction.

"Well ... at least he ain't dead," Bill replied. "Though he did a pretty good job of trying to do himself in on that horse."

Jim glanced at the ground and just shook his head. Bill was a tough boss to work for and usually right about most things, this being one of them. He should have put the kid on a gentler mount to see if he could ride or not. That was his problem ... he put too much faith in what others told him. Bill was just the opposite. He could read others like a book and knew instantly by their mannerisms and speech just what kind of person he was dealing with. He was blunt and to the point—leaving little doubt about how he felt. Jim played the diplomat and Bill ... well; Bill never "played" nothing. Bill was all business.

"Jim, I'll tell you what we're going to do for this kid when we get there, providing his brain ain't too scrambled from his *near-death* experience—damn I ain't seen nobody fly like that since *Superman*! I'm going to make sure he's alright—without letting on so, and then if he's okay … I'm going to rip him a new ass for letting one of my horses get away. If he in any way shirks, I'm going to fire him on the spot! If he stands up and says that he can't ride worth a damn and that he's sorry for letting the horse get away, and that he'll do better next time … then we'll keep him for the time being. How's that sound to you, Jim?"

"Sounds alright by me," Jim answered.

"Good! Now, about that paperwork."

"What paperwork?"

"I swear to God you've got the shortest memory of anybody I know. I'm talking about that damn resume!"

"What about the resume?"

"I want you to give it back to the kid and tell him to update that part about his horse experience."

Jim replied, "You got it Bill."

"Oh…. Jim there's something else you need to explain to this kid about that piece of paper."

"What's that, Bill?"

"Tell the kid that after he's done rewriting it where he can put it."

Jim glanced sideways at his boss with complete understanding. Bill glanced back with a smile and devilment in his eye.

He reached into his breast pocket for his cigarettes and muttered, "*Modern Times*! The hell you say!"

DISTANT VISTAS

This land swells, falls, and then rolls away towards distant vistas. Puffy clouds that drift across azure skies and the wind … always the wind—lessens to a gentle touch that barely extracts the day's temperature from one's body. The mid-afternoon sun makes this land simmer with the heat rising in waves that are seen at ground level. Riding upon a high swell on this ocean of grass, miles distant I see a clump of greenery that can only be cottonwood trees and a source of water indicating the whereabouts of ranch buildings in this broad and expansive land we have named Wyoming—an oasis to retire to at day's end. Tourist season and visitors seeking the west's majestic scenery, travel the interstates, lured by brochures of things to do and places to visit. A hundred miles to the southwest I can make out the Colorado Rocky Mountains capped with heavenly peaks of snow, and I contemplate extremes.

No motorized vehicle can transport one to pamphlet prophesies. It can only be done by horseback—for seeing is feeling and one cannot feel this land from inside an automobile. No camera is capable of producing a Kodiak moment that can capture the magnitude of this country. No words can give vision to the mind, though I continually attempt to do so. Sagebrush, prickly pear and soap weed mingle with rocky outcrops and grassy plains. Horse flesh, sweat and leather—my natural cologne for the day. I smell of this land and become one with the sky above and the horse's gait beneath me. Rusty barbed wire and petrified fence posts that transposes into distant nothingness and a song in the wire.

I grasp it … but I cannot hold it—only share it with my inner self, as I have periodically done for these past thirty-seven years. I am like an old dog traveling down a gravel road searching for new sights and promising adventures. Then I come limping home years later with stories of distant lands and a faraway life. I seek familiarity and comfort—solace for the soul. This land is my liquor like bourbon whisky that rinses the dust and eases aching muscles—not indulgence but a palate pleaser that beckons another after the first shot glass is finished. Sometimes the soul must be emptied before it can be replenished.

A faint cry of the circling hawk above carries my ascending thoughts upwards where there are no boundaries—no fences, just the unending and untouchable sky. I learned to float before I could swim … and now I'm floating again. This prairie ocean has a great Instructor, and I've attempted to learn the lessons he has imparted upon me. Swimming requires effort but floating demands patience and allowing one's body to seek equilibrium. Perhaps that is what I'm doing here—seeking equilibrium without strife. It cannot last … this floating on the vast openness.

The smoothest part of the ride is full gallop. To me there is rhythm of movement and balance of horse and rider that flattens the rough area ahead. I feel the rush … the pounding of the horse's hoofs and the speed that danger beckons before me. Onward! Onward … towards distant vistas, and I am carried away.

ADRIEN SERRANT

Adrien Serrant's home is France. He is here working this summer and appears to be enjoying his stay at the Cattail Ranch. Adrien has thus far endured most of the same hardships and work that others have endured, but he has done so with a certain French inquisitiveness in our American western culture. Only nineteen years of age, he will return to France soon and hopefully tell wonderful stories to his family and friends about his cowboy experiences here at the ranch and this home we call Wyoming.

I was around Adrien's age when I arrived here the first time. First impressions are lasting impressions. The lure of the cowboy life, wide-open skies, the climate and friendly folks all spoke to me at various times in my lifetime … and I came back. Adrien's sister, Emily, was here working at the ranch a few summers ago. She is now twenty-two and has obviously related her experiences to her younger brother. There have been others from France in years past who have lived and worked here. Like it or not, we are all brothers and sisters in the international community. How we communicate with one another, the treatment of others and our mannerisms, and the friendships we form—all determine our American "character" as viewed by the rest of the world.

This morning I shanghaied Adrien and took him to Cheyenne with me. I had a few things I needed to accomplish in town but the primary purpose of this excursion was to make sure Adrien had the cowboy hat he wanted. Craig footed the entire cost of the hat and I provided the means to insure Adrien found his hat and the other souvenirs that he wanted. I reckoned the best way to accomplish this mission was for Adrien to hightail it out of here before anyone had a say about his absence from work, so we left at six-thirty this morning. Adrien was worried that Rod would be angry at him for not showing up for work this morning. I told him not to worry—Rod would understand that Adrien was in the good company of the best renegade around. Besides, it might have been a few years ago that Rod was nineteen but I was sure he could still remember back to his youth and he would understand, though I'm not so sure that Adrien understood this explanation.

I bought breakfast for the two of us at Perkins Restaurant. Adrien sure likes that sugary stuff for his morning meal. I stayed with an omelet, hash browns, muffin and black coffee. Adrien, on the other hand, had banana pancakes, hot chocolate, and a big glass of orange juice. Must be a French thing. We had a good breakfast conversation. We talked about the differences in our countries. I told him about my experiences when I traveled through France and about the folks I met along the way. He talked of his home, work, education and his family. We both enjoyed swimming in the Mediterranean Sea off the coast of Spain. (Both of us agreed that the Atlantic coast was much too cold for any enjoyable swimming.)

Similarities and differences ... woven into the web of life. Old man and youth—discovering common ground.

We left and I finished the few things I needed to do in town, then we headed on over to Corral West Ranchwear in search of a cowboy hat. Adrien tried on nearly every damn hat in that store, as I maintained the patience of Job. But after awhile, he finally found the hat he was looking for. A nice-looking, black cowboy hat with a wide brim that fit just right. He flicked the front brim of his hat a few times to make sure that hat wouldn't be too loose on his head. He checked himself out several times in that old mirror. "That's the one, Adrien," I said. "Yes," he replied with a smile. "A good-looking hat too," I told him. All I saw though ... was a young cowboy.

COLD WATER

Tearing out beaver dams out in the Swifts Saturday. It was cold and windy—snow on the ground and ice across many portions of the fast-moving stream. The beaver have this insane tendency to build where they are least welcomed. At least there are still beaver here on the ranch. Big critters too! I was on the south side of the bank trying to create an opening in one of the dams so as to divert the water more to the south. I had hip waders on along with my normal "seasonal" clothing consisting of long underwear, bandana, gloves, and coat with a winter hat and flaps over my ears. After accomplishing the task of opening this particular section of the beaver dam I quickly found out that the opening I had created was now letting so much water through that I could no longer cross back over the way I had previously come. I started down the south bank in search of a more suitable crossing that was not as deep or swift. I found myself on a thin shelf of ice along the bank. Trying to maintain my balance on ice and water is not an easy task for me. (Anything that gets between my feet and the ground usually has me upside down in no time—the one exception is horses.) A muffled explosion preceded my immediate decent into the cold and murky waters as the ice gave way. My waders (which reached to my hips) immediately filled with water as I quickly found myself in water up to my chest. Struggling to maintain my balance I was immediately knocked of my feet by the current and slabs of ice and now found a new water depth that reached up to my neck. Any previous thought of departing this water hole with only the lower half of me wet were quickly dispatched. I could not regain my feet in the swift current and with everything but my head under water, my clothing and waders soon had assumed the role of an effective anchor. By now I figured what the hell, I might as well try and make it to the north bank.

I still had the long iron hook in one hand that I had used to tear apart the beaver dam. The only equipment I really need by now was a snorkel. Rod and Barbie were way off to the eastern end of the Swifts pasture about five-hundred yards distance with the tractor and one truck filling in another portion of the stream bank. Craig had already preceded me in getting one of his waders filled with water and had headed on back in the other truck to the ranch proper several miles distant to change out of his clothes. I pulled my upper body up across the thin ice and immediately broke through again. The next attempt proved more successful and I was finally able to pull myself up over the bank. The brisk wind and cold temperature quickly let me know that I was still alive because I felt every bit of both! I attempted to unbuckle the waders from my belt but my hands were going numb. I was all thumbs—and I couldn't even feel them. Finally, I sat down on the snow and pulled the waders off and emptied several gallons of water from each. I slipped both waders back on and made my way to Rod and Barbie's location. Ten minutes later I was sitting inside the truck out of the wind and feeling a little better now that I had taken my bath for the day.

Barbie drove me in the truck back to my home, which we reached in about forty-five minutes. I found that my clothing was turning to ice. After several attempts I was finally able to get all of my clothes off and myself into a hot shower. (Barbie was not there for this event.) I know now why I like hot water much more so than cold water.

There must be a moral to this story. Perhaps it is, "Don't skate on thin ice." Or, "You don't have to practice to be miserable." It could be that you "shouldn't play with beavers or their dams, or the damn beavers—period!" At any rate, I've located an excellent swimming hole for next summer.

NEWS STORIES

Calving season is here at the Cattail Ranch. I was in Cheyenne today and while in town I browsed the *Denver Post*. I read a couple of articles of interest to me. One of the articles dealt with the subject of Mad Cow Disease. I enjoy reading "statistics" and this one article had a few concerning the beef industry. Of particular interest were the figures concerning the number of cattle slaughtered here in the United States for meat consumption. Somewhere in the neighborhood of 34 million head of cattle a year ends up on someone's dinner table either here in America or elsewhere in the world. The article further cited that in that total there was one confirmed case of Mad Cow Disease, which was imported from our "friendly" neighbor to the north—Canada. Of course, that one cow sure did spin the meat market out of control for the American ranchers. Japan has been a large buyer of American meat and the Japanese now want every head of cattle to be tested for Mad Cow Disease before the beef is exported to their country. Now, I never was too good at math (I don't even attempt to balance my check book without the aid of a calculator), but it seems to me that one bad cow out of 34 million good cuds appears to be darn safe for putting beef on the table without too much worry. I don't know anyone who eats cow brains anyway. (Why mess with the head when there's so much meat on the rest of the bovine?) I'd rather eat beef than "Yard Bird" (slang for chicken) and more people get sick and die from eating bad bird than eating mad moo.

The problem is serious when it affects ranching operations. Of course, this scare shook the American meat market. Japan's request that cattle be tested for Mad Cow Disease will cost around $20.00 dollars per head—something that will definitely hurt the individual rancher who is trying to just make ends meet. The cost far outweighs the risk incurred. I don't know about you but if I had one bad dollar out of 34 million dollars I sure wouldn't bother with the calculator. (The IRS might—but I sure as hell wouldn't worry about it.) I'd tell the Japanese that if they didn't want to buy our beef to look elsewhere in the world for a "safer" provider (they won't find one) than the American cattle producer. So, what's the beef?

Another article in the *Denver Post* dealt with the water levels of Lake Powell and Lake Mead. The water level of these two bodies of water is presently at 42% capacity. (The mighty Colorado River doesn't even make it to the ocean any longer due to the demands of water usage.) And as if the drought isn't bad enough, we have all of the various states' attorneys haggling over the legal ramifications of who owns what portion of that water supply. The article stated that if things don't improve quickly that by 2005 there won't be any water in those two lakes for anyone's use! America's present population explosion will create more demand than supply and that spells trouble in our own backyard. It seems to me that the only ones that can get us out of the drought situation are the lawyers. Anyway, it looks good on paper. (I'd place more faith in my own rain dance than I would a bunch of legal criminals, thank you.)

The last article I read was about the running of the bulls in Spain. Again there were more statistics regarding the number of deaths and injuries from being gored by a bull over there in Spain (Something like America almost got in the last presidential election—"Gored"). I have to tell you folks that running from a mad bull that can lift three times his own weight with his head is not my kind of "fun". As a matter of fact, I don't find anything humorous about bulls. (We have a lot more bad bulls than mad juicers in this country.) The only "sport" in running with the bulls is for the bulls themselves. I just don't feel too sporty when I have a bull chasing me—but I sure as hell feel athletic though. And that's no bull!

So there you have it folks. Stories from demented doggies to dried-up watering holes; and on to the "gory" sport of real-life horn-honking—all in one day's newspaper. Is it any wonder that Americans are tired of today's headline news? All you have to do is turn a few pages to get to the real stories. I never found the comics page.

HORSES AND WEATHER

I rode Chief yesterday helping move cattle out of the Gusher and over into the Three Windmills range. Today I rode Lollipop when we brought in some pairs of mothers with calves that needed branding. Chief never walks—I don't believe that "walking" is even in his vocabulary. I incurred my share of saddle chafing from Chief, even though I was wearing my chaps. Today I took it easy on myself with Lollipop, who is a much gentler and smarter horse. I reckon that getting smarter comes with age. I'll ride Chief again when I get some more skin grafted back on my legs. I only had one calf that I branded today whose mark just wasn't "artistic" enough for me. But any day that I'm not in town working is a blessing to me.

These last five days we've seen some much-needed rainfall. It's been good moisture alternating between downpours to steady drizzles. Today it's sunny and warmer and the grass is greening up again. I got to thinking about weather and horses and the similarities between the two. Both are unpredictable, temperamental and can knock you out when they have a mind to. Then again both can be beautiful, warm and gentle when you need them the most. When working in town I lose "touch" with the things that mean the most to me. I get surly and agitated. I want to tell the boss to take his job and shove it "where the sun don't shine". But it pays my bills. I wouldn't have any bills if I'd stop spending money. But then I wouldn't have spent the money in the first place unless I thought I needed what I was buying. (There's buyer's logic in that statement somewhere.) I've known folks who would buy something whether they needed it or not—because it was a real bargain. The way I figure it is that it ain't a bargain if you don't need it. Ranching would better suit my disposition but it would be tough trying to make ends meet. I really shouldn't complain too much because in a way, I have the best of both worlds. It's just that the "other" world—the city life, chaffs me more than Chief does.

I purchased a book for Michel titled *Downsize This* written by Michael Moore. In his book Moore is critical of how the corporations run America. He's not too fond of the Bush administration either. I'll read the book when Michel is done reading it—she cuts me no slack in letting me know her feelings are aligned with those of Mr. Moore when she reads certain passages of the book to me. Politicians are like horses and weather—they all have the rear anatomy of a horse and they change their political views depending on which way the wind is blowing. My political leanings have the characteristics of both Republicans and Democrats. I'm employed by a Republican Fortune-Five-Hundred Corporation (Lowe's is now in the top fifty of the Fortune-Five-Hundred) in order to have an income—then I turn around and blow my hard-earned dollars, just like a Democrat. I reckon that makes me an "All-American".

I would lean more to the Democrat side if they weren't so anti-gun and willing to spend my tax dollars on everything that came along. Then again I would be more inclined to be a Republican if they weren't so big on corporations and would let some of that money trickle down to the pockets of those doing the actual work. I guess I'll just remain an Independent. I wish we had an election where instead of voting someone into office we could vote the ones we didn't like out of office. After awhile there wouldn't be any government at all—we'd all be better off and a whole lot richer in the process.

What this country needs is another Theodore Roosevelt. I liked Teddy's philosophy of "Walk softly but carry a big stick". He didn't mince words when it came time for action—he just knocked them up alongside the head and they got the message. Teddy was an avid outdoors man, a cattleman and cowboy, a hunter, an environmentalist. He was fond of good weaponry, rode horses and was a Rough Rider, and he wasn't concerned about making enemies. He was a politician, but he didn't pull his punches. I visited his ranch near Medora, North Dakota over in the badland area several years ago. The setting is rustic in that rough part of the country. I believe that we are what we live our lives by—the setting provides the scenario. I think that Teddy's ranch setting had a lot to do with his scenario later on in life. Like horses and weather, you just have to take the good with the bad—and deal with it.

HOT IRON

Forty-five … forty-four … forty-three … Heat that singes the face and wind that sends coals spiraling like hot shrapnel towards my feet and smoke that makes my eyes water. *Hot Iron!* I call out as I walk towards the next calf. My gloved hands holding the branding iron, with two additional leather gloves cushioning the middle portion of the iron and the smell of burning hair and hide as I apply the iron to the calf's side. Smoke fills the air and I can't see as the iron burns through the hair and imprints the mark of the "Pitcher" brand on the hide. Forty-two … forty-one … I add more wood to the fire pit to keep the five irons from cooling. "Heifer" is called out and I grab the Number "4" iron for the little Hereford's left hind rump. Four iron of the year she was born—2004. Today it's cooler because of the rain we had last night. The wind soothes my face and my beard and clears the smoke from my eyes. Forty … thirty-nine … damn, I didn't like that last brand mark—the calf was tossing around making it difficult to get a "clean" mark. I take pride in attempting to accomplish a clean brand and I am upset with myself for making more than one burn line. *Damn you Jordan … concentrate on a clean burn and roll that iron with the calf's movement!* I think to myself. Sometimes it works, and then sometimes it doesn't. Thirty-eight—it's a good brand, this time.

I'm not making my "mark" … but the ranch's mark when I brand. Branding has been done here since the 1800's and throughout the western United States for an even longer time period. Ownership of the cattle must be established; otherwise they'll become the property of others. "Rustling" is an old business and can be profitable with the present-day technology that is currently available. Forget the old "round 'em up" and "move 'em out" technique. Today, it's just a matter of backing the tractor-trailer rig towards a holding area and loading the cattle. Then take the back roads out and be well out of the area in just a few hours today—that would have required several days to do so by horseback years ago, and a greater chance of discovery in the process.

Thirty-seven … I enjoy hearing the lonesome Morning Dove cooing in the trees above our home during the early morning hours. Shortly before the sun crests the eastern horizon—the dewy grass and Cottonwood leaves flutter to the music of dove and the morning breeze's whisper. *Okay boys … let's break out the bugle and sound reveille, for a new day is about to commence.* Silence. I can handle that too—Nature's orchestra is winding up. Twenty-three … I'm hotter than a fart in a skillet, as I stir the coals and add more wood to the fire. They've got another calf ready for me as I change out another burnt glove before grabbing the next iron. "Chief" gave me a pretty good ride this morning. That horse is as crazy as I am—so I let him have the reigns a couple of times so he could run as hard as he wanted to go. When a horse sticks his neck and tail straight out and reaches out for the ground in front of him … you know you're going into "autopilot". *Let 'er rip Chief—you crazy bastard! It's just you and me ol' boy!* Ride like the wind … and don't ever look back. I need a tighter fitting saddle—I figure about a fourteen-inch would be just right for me. Fourteen … I lift the iron as the hair briefly flares up in fire, then place the hot iron back to the calf's side. A decent mark—could have done better, so I'll keep on trying to improve my skills.

"Heifer"—and I grab the Number "4" iron. Chief rubs his head against my backside and pushes me as we walk along towards the horse barn. *Yea … that's right ol' boy—we're both just a bit touched in the head.* Nine … and I'm up on the western windmill out at the Sheep Camp. The brake doesn't work, and so the fan blades turn with the slightest breeze as I crawl beneath their movement and I pull myself onto the platform. Not quick enough, one of the fan blades catches me and slices a two-inch cut in my back. But I'm up here now and I ain't going down till the job is done. I can't find the damn foot-peg so I stand on the cross beams at the top of the tower to get the cover off and to refill the oil in the gear box. *I reckon that this is about as close to Heaven as I'll ever get. I've already done my time in Hell so anything else would be an improvement.* Now I can't get the cover aligned so as to drop it back over housing. I've got both of my legs wrapped around this steel tower so as to use both of my hands to align things—finally, everything fits into place.

Five … damn near set another calf on fire again. I lift the iron as the smoke from burning hair is so thick I can't see what I'm doing. That damn cut where the fan blade got me is hurting now. The Collins windmill needs some repairing. A rivet has busted loose from the hold-down arm that shuts the mill off. I cut a bolt too short so now I'm down on the ground again cutting another bolt. My fingers are black from the greasy oil as I try to get the bolt and nut to thread once more up above. I had to climb up on this platform from the outside of the tower because the fan blades were right above my head and I couldn't get up all the way using the ladder. I tighten the nut and bolt with my ratchet and ½ inch wrench. Finally everything is tight … and my wrench drops out of my coveralls to somewhere on the ground below. It takes me a half hour to find it again. Back on the ground and I splice the broken cable around the water tank.

Last calf! … Where have I been? Evening ushers the slightest breeze as the sun drops behind the western horizon and the first star twinkles. Night sounds and the "whirly birds" as I call them begin their tune in the trees above me. Night

Birds. The chopper props thump the grass and ground about me … whop, whop, whop—*Churn it up boys—and give 'em Hell! Get a grip, Jordan … the war's over for you boy.* Yea right—but it ain't over for the one's still doing their duty for mom, country and apple pie. *Chief … you crazy bastard—I think you and I are going to get along just fine.* I grab one of the branding irons that I'll use for the last time this day and walk towards the last calf. Somewhere along the way I sound off with … *Hot Iron!*

A ROAD TO SOMEWHERE

Overhead the thunder crashes, coupled with flashes of lightening illuminating the yard and the wind constantly changing directions. At times a cold breeze blows through the windows and rattles the screen door of our home. The power cuts out and momentary blackness prevails. Just as quickly the lights come back on with the accompaniment of more lightening and thunder. Jagged streaks arc through the night sky creating a moist and wonderful freshness in the air. By this morning the storm has passed, leaving cooler temperatures and a light soaking rain falling from gray clouds.

The drive to Denver this morning takes me along the muddy gravel roads and wet asphalt until I arrive at the Colorado border. I'm visiting with my daughter and getting away for while. I've left the ranch, my job and Michel behind me. It's time for thought and a time for direction. I've worked hard all of my life and I've earned only more work in the process. Work rewarded with more work and in the end, nothing gained except more pain and mental anguish. This past Thursday I requested a leave of absence from my employer until December. My request was approved. Maybe I'll go back.

At times I wonder just what a job is worth. How much crap in the workplace is worth digesting? Sure, there are good days and bad days, but when every day is a lousy day it's difficult to distinguish the difference between "tolerance" and "acceptance". Amanda and I watched the movie *Gladiator* this afternoon here at her apartment. I had seen the film before but I needed a further definition of slavery. At least working at Lowe's as a slave isn't a life or death situation … just humiliation. So far, I have been in good company with all of the other slaves working there. The difference is that I recognize slavery for what it is, while others are content with being humiliated for a paycheck.

When I arrived in Denver this morning I intended to stop for breakfast at Perkins Restaurant located at Sheridan Boulevard and 84th Street. I missed my turn-off and ended up heading for downtown. I finally found another street and turned around, but I couldn't get to Perkins because there were no streets that I could take in that direction. Forty-five minutes later and still hungry, I finally gave up trying to find a route and decided to say to hell with it and drove to my daughter's apartment instead. (Fortunately, we decided on going out for an early lunch.) In Denver, when I can't see the mountains or the sun I have no idea which direction I'm heading. Maybe that's my problem. No mountains worth climbing and no sunlight to brighten one's perspective. No direction to travel.

Tonight, as I sit at this table beside an open window and type away on this laptop of mine, I can hear the crickets outside. I haven't heard any crickets at the ranch this summer and I think it odd that I must drive to a major metropolitan area such as Denver to hear crickets. Things, other than me, seem out of place. There's a nice cool breeze without any effort of wind. It's quite here tonight too with little automobile traffic outside. Amanda calls Thomas in Jacksonville Beach, Florida and asks him if he is okay now that Hurricane Frances is just hours away. He tells her that the wind is picking up speed and the hurricane is due to arrive there at two o'clock tomorrow (Sunday) morning. Thomas tells her they're supposed to get at least a foot of rain and that he presently has no plans to evacuate his sea-side apartment. And why would he? Here's a young man who climbs mountains alone, parachutes from airplanes, who accepts the stings of jellyfish and swims in the company of sharks while in search of the next big wave. He gives real meaning to that youthful phrase of *No Fear*. I must have done something right in raising my son and daughter.

Amanda and I return from Starbucks. I bought coffee for Mike and myself. Amanda doesn't drink coffee and there's none available here at their apartment. I'm enjoying the company of Amanda and her fiancé Mike. Outside it is now raining and the crickets have ceased their nocturnal melody for the moment. Mike has his computer online competing with other contestants in a game, while Amanda is playing with their cats. It's a little after 9:00 p.m. when I finally phone Michel back at the ranch. She and the dogs are doing fine and it is raining there too. She's had a hard day at work today and she has another long day ahead of her again tomorrow.

I think about how I got here this morning and the distance I covered. Way up north towards the direction of Wyoming I see lightening illuminating the clouds and it has stopped raining here. The crickets are busy once more and a cool breeze reaches me when I step outside onto the balcony to take a break from writing. My Starbucks coffee cup is empty but the old mental processes are still grinding away. Today, when Amanda and I stopped at the Barnes & Noble bookstore,

I bought four books for Michel authored by Carlos Castaneda. Michel is an avid reader but had not read any of his works. I had previously given a brief synopsis to her about his writings and she was interested in obtaining some of his books. I thought she might enjoy his writings since many of the stories took place in the American southwest where Michel grew up and in Mexico. I have not read any of Carlos' books since the early seventies. It will be nice to reacquaint myself with his writings once Michel is finished reading them.

All roads lead to somewhere. Presently, I'm still on the road, if only in thought. I've always enjoyed traveling to distant places. If I could modestly afford to do so, I would enjoy traveling and writing about my encounters with other folks. But I would always need a home to come home to. (Even the traveler needs a break once in awhile.) Tomorrow I'll leave Denver and supposedly return to the ranch. But there are many paths between here and there. Many paths that, should I choose to do so, I can follow and just loose myself. I wouldn't be lost. I'd just go away … to somewhere, and return again … someday. This time if it looks like a good road … I just may take it.

LOVE IS NEVER WASTED

Love is never wasted. Talk about a unique statement! Those very words were given to me this evening over the phone from Michel. What a wonderful gift she shared with this battered old boy! She tells me to begin writing again … at least a paragraph. So, here's my attempt at cranking up the old mental processes once more. Months ago I had seriously thought about writing a novel for my next book. That changed when I moved back here to the ranch, and I thought that maybe I should write about the ranch instead. I've put both projects on hold for the present time. Instead, I've decided to write about things closer to me. When I wrote *Considerations—Emails From the Heart* it took an accumulation of several years and some prodding to eventually put it all together. Now I'm being prodded by Michel to begin writing again. (Like Merrill-Lynch … when Michel speaks, I listen.)

Perhaps I could blend the three subjects of a novel, the ranch and Michel—that way I'll have a book consisting of fiction, reality … and a fairytale. (Michel would tell me that I have the sequence of the last three messed-up—as usual.) It would be a best-seller and I could retire and do something worthwhile like riding a horse without looking at the rear end of some ornery cattle in front of me. Don't get me wrong here … some rear ends are worth looking at! (Even cowboys have a taste for the better things in life.) But it would be nice doing something worthwhile for a change. I might even make a couple of million dollars from the book. I'm not a financial wizard but I know that if I rub two five-dollar bills together long enough that I'll eventually have ten bucks.

My son calls me and says the temperatures have been back in the eighties there in Florida. Good surfing weather. My daughter emails me and says that she and her fiancé are back together now. (I told her, "Good job Punkin! I'm proud of you ... so very proud! You have guts! Get a grip on your life and grab Mike by the gonads and live it up. You're my daughter—and always will be! I love you to pieces! You have a special place in my heart ... and always will.") Last week she had told me that her nineteen year old cat, Butterball, had to be put down. Now she is starting life again. That's the beauty of living, whether you're waiting for the next big wave or just what's around the corner—it just keeps on getting better. And if it's not getting better for you ... then you're just not looking in the right places. I know where my "place" is and I'm comfortable there. "Intense" maybe ... but still comfortable. However, I'm still hoping to become more comfortable in the very near future. That is of course if ... *Love is never wasted.*

DOGGIE FUN

Kelly likes to rug surf. Throw his ball in the air and he's bounding across the kitchen floor in hot pursuit. The kitchen rugs are his vehicle of transportation and are scattered about the kitchen floor as if a Wyoming twister had just hit the place. "Dog-Proofing" is a tough job.

When the "Boys" arrived here with Michel I was hard-pressed identifying remedies for a number of "incidents" of misbehavior (otherwise known in the dog world as "Doggie Fun"). When the boys were left alone here at the house without human intervention they went to work right away. Bucky always headed for the kitchen trash can and proceeded to extract any paper or cardboard products and shred them—scattering the pieces throughout the household. (It kind of looked like your lawn when you're cutting the grass and run over a newspaper with the lawnmower.) I "Dog-Proofed" the trash can by placing it in the cupboard under the kitchen sink where he couldn't get to it anymore. Success. Yea, right! Bucky found the trash can in the bathroom and was back to his old self again. So, I put that trash can in the bathroom cupboard. So far, so good.

The kitchen table was located by the kitchen window—a superb lookout platform for Kelly. I would enter the house and find him standing on the kitchen table as the ever-watchful sentinel. I decided to move the kitchen table away from the window and to the center of the kitchen floor. (I'd teach Kelly that standing on the kitchen table and looking out the window for our arrival would not be tolerated!) So I would arrive home and Kelly would be standing on the kitchen table—now in the middle of the kitchen. (He could still see out the kitchen window.) So the kitchen table is now in the center of the kitchen and as we leave the house we close the curtains at the kitchen window. This is working—so far.

Other forms of doggie fun for Kelly and Bucky include raiding the other ranch house yards of bones or anything else of doggie interest. These "raids" are usually conducted under the cover of darkness when the other ranch dogs are inside and unaware that their "stash" is about to be lifted. Of course, all of that "loot" is brought back to our house and deposited on the floor as newly found "bounty". A couple of days ago this seized treasure included a sizeable calf hipbone that Kelly is still gnawing on in the middle of our living room floor. This is ranch life at its best! (I have to be so careful when I get out of bed in the middle of the night and walk barefoot across the floor that I don't trip over a recently acquired carcass.)

Like humans, Kelly and Bucky have their own individual characteristics. Bucky—the Sheltie/Husky mix was born in 1991. Kelly—the Australian Sheppaid, was born in 1999. Bucky is an old dog now and cannot hear well (or so he says). He also has arthritis. Kelly is still a kid—and lives the juvenile life. Both dogs are keen on making their bed wherever we humans sleep. It's not unusual to find yourself awakened in the middle of the night with an Australian Sheppard straddling your prone body and his nose to your nose with a ball in his mouth ready to play. "Not now, Kelly! Get off of me you big lug!" Kelly is a great back support when both of us do sleep. Bucky seeks attention and reassurance by barking while Michel and I are trying to converse with one another. "Jealousy" is his middle name. (Talk about a three-way conversation!) He's a good curler in bed though. He tends to plop down on the pillow next to my head when I'm getting ready to sleep and I have to move him to my feet so that I don't commit some form of self-induced fur-ball suicide.

There are other little idiosyncrasies that I have learned to cope with. When Michel and I arrive back at the ranch in the morning from a night's work the whole household goes nuts. Both dogs are barking and running back and forth, excited at our arrival. The kitchen rugs go flying across the kitchen floor, dog toys are gathered in mouths (theirs—not ours), tails swish the previous day's dust deposits from every nook and cranny in the house and total bedlam prevails. It is nice to be appreciated. And then it's out the door for necessary relief (again, theirs—not ours).

No dog will ever replace my Tippy. But both of these canines have filled that certain emptiness in my heart that I have endured for these past several years. My home will never quite be the same again. You could call this home of ours *Animal House*. Or you could name it *The Zoo*. Or you could say that it's just plain ... Doggie Fun.

DISTANT THUNDER

Yesterday evening, I drove up the road about three-and-a-half miles to the shooting shack here at the ranch. I took my Remington Model 700 ADL Synthetic and twenty rounds of factory 30.06 ammo. I wanted to check the zero on my rifle. While walking out to recover my first target I came across a rattlesnake four feet from me. I had just traveled this same route fifteen minutes earlier so I was a little surprised to have a rattler where I had previously walked. Walking around this temporary obstacle, I changed out my target, and then carefully made my way back to the shooting shack, ever mindful that where there is one rattler there is probably another one nearby.

Far off to the west I could hear the distant sound of thunder. Seconds later I added my own thunder when I let go another round. After firing ten rounds my right shoulder was beginning to feel the effects. Twenty rounds later my shoulder was getting stiff. Off in the west I could hear another comforting sound of thunder. Statistics for the 165 grain Winchester Super X Pointed Soft Point 30.06 bullet I'm firing shows that I have a muzzle velocity of 2,800 fps (feet-per-second). At 500 yards that same bullet still has 1,151 ft. lbs. (foot-pounds) of energy. At that distance it's the equivalent of having a half-ton of knock-down power at 1,772 feet-per-second. When zeroed at 200 yards, this same bullet has a long-range trajectory of -49.6 inches at 500 yards, so sight alignment and trajectory is critical. I still favor the 30.06 over the .308 round that our military utilizes today.

When compared with the present .308 Winchester (7.62 x 51mm NATO) round the 30.06 Springfield (7.62 x 63mm NATO) is a far more efficient sniper round. At 1,000 yards the ballistics between the two is even more diverse. Using a 168 grain bullet comparison for both calibers at 1,000 yards the .308 has a velocity of 1,168.8 feet-per-second, 509.6 foot-pounds of energy, with a -394.4 drop in inches. The 30.06 on the other hand has a velocity 1,296.7 feet-per-second,

627.3 foot-pounds of energy, with a -315.5 drop in inches. In the past, our efforts to standardize ammunition with our NATO allies resulted in the United States short-changing itself in ballistics while at the same time increasing the profits of the arms and ammunition manufacturers. Politics prevailed over common sense and the efficient, time-proven ballistics of the 30.06 Springfield round.

Things haven't changed much today. Our government's "standardization" policies and procurement of junk to arm today's soldier threatens their very lives on the battlefield. We may have our high-tech weapons and delivery systems, but it is the soldier on the ground that takes possession and wins the war. It's done with mud, blood and guts. We are fast approaching that "magical" number of 1,000 KIA's in Iraq—and for what? For some camel jockey that hasn't a clue of what constitutes a real democracy, and who could care less. It's more fun to bushwhack and kill American soldiers.

Not one man or woman in today's Army is a draftee. They're all volunteers who have taken an oath to defend and protect the Constitution of the United States. And yet this administration continually places them in harm's way and equips them with inadequate weapons and leadership—then hangs them out to dry with extended tours of enlistments and subsequent rotations into Iraq.

With the naked eye at one-thousand yards, I cannot see the one-inch grids on my target, or the holes each bullet prints on paper. But at one-thousand yards I know I can hit a bureaucrat's desk … and savor the sound of his distant thunder.

TUMBLEWEED

Tumbleweed. The wind blows and they come alive, frolicking along at ground level. Sometimes they hit an obstacle in their path and go airborne for some distance before landing to begin their summersaults again. That's what I have done many times in my lifetime—played the tumbleweed role. Going the direction the wind blows me and then, when I hit an obstacle, going to flight until I land head-over-heels and continue bouncing along in another new direction. The four things I never know for sure are—how much the wind will blow, how high I will fly, where I might land next, and in what new direction I'll be heading. At least it keeps life interesting for me. Once in awhile I'll snag myself on something and stay put for a longer period of time, just like the tumbleweed. I've often wondered what becomes of the tumbleweed when it has reached its life expectancy.

Does it just disintegrate into pieces or does it become something more tangible—like another tumbleweed somewhere down the line?

Here at the ranch my time is preoccupied mostly with work, leaving little time for reading and more importantly, writing. It's hard for me to concentrate on anything else when Michel is actually here. (I do a lot of concentrating on Michel … and I'm sure not complaining about that!) But I need more time to read and write and to pursue other interests. We enjoy living here at the ranch away from the bustling city life, but I miss interacting with "civilization" on a more frequent basis. I'm a social animal that enjoys my privacy, if you can imagine that! The other day while I was "tumbling" along the wind came up and whispered in my ear. She said words to the effect that: *Ranching is okay and being a poor Cowboy is a wonderful life, but son you need to get going in another direction if you're ever going to pay off your bills and get that book of yours written. I mean, I know you love the West, cowboy hats and boots, horses and the sweet smell of cow shit in the morning. But you need to interact with civilization again. I know you've got a wonderful little gal and things are looking rosy but damn it boy … you need to get a grip!*

The wind got my attention and bounced me up in the air and sent me flying off in another direction … kind of. I began mulling things over and being the impulsive person that I am I decided that: *What the hell … why can't I do it all?* So I made a decision. I decided that Michel and I will continue to maintain our home here at the ranch and that I will return to work at the Lowe's Regional Distribution Center in Cheyenne. A couple of days ago I began the re-hire process with Lowe's and worked out the necessary details to maintain our residence here at the Cattail Ranch. I finished-up the preliminaries with Lowe's this afternoon and I am to report back to work on the night shift next week. Since both Michel and I will be working the night shift for the same employer we'll be able to utilize one vehicle and travel back and forth together. The winter weather route is 104 miles round-trip. If the weather improves the route will be shorter. (That way I can sleep when I'm driving and Michel can watch the road for me.)

I'll have more weekends off (except when we go into overtime status next month at Lowe's) and I'll be able to "pester" other civilized folks other than Michel. (She needs the break.) I can pay off my bills, get that book written, wear my cowboy hat and boots, ride the horses, and still savor the sweet smell of cow shit in the mornings.

I don't know just what this tumbleweed will become when I've reached my life expectancy. But, I hope to keep bouncing along until then. I hope the cattle don't get a hankering to eat this tumbleweed … because I'll know what I'll become!

HAYING OPERATIONS

Every morning during the winter the cattle need hay to supplement their meager grass supply. The amount of effort that goes into just getting the hay to the cattle is phenomenal. Around July the hay here at the ranch is ready for cutting. (We call it "hay" but it isn't near the quality of hay as we know it back in the Midwestern sections of our country. It is mostly grass.) The cutting is accomplished with a cycle mower mounted on the three-point hitch of a tractor. The flattened hay is left to dry for at least one day. Sometimes it rains after cutting so this lengthens the time element. Next, a wheel rake is used to place the hay into wind rows so that another tractor with the baler can proceed along the rows and bale the hay into round bales. Each "native grass" bale of hay weighs approximately 900 pounds when it is "kicked-out" of the baler. Another tractor comes along pulling a "Tumble Bug" backs this equipment to the round bale and drops the forks into the bale and onto a frame and then the bale is transported to the stack yard. Dump rakes are pulled behind yet other tractors to gather up loose hay still left on the ground after the baler has gone through. The hay is gathered up in the teeth and then "dumped" into new rows for the baler once more. The bales are stored outside on top of one another inside a fenced area (the stack yard). This is accomplished with the use of another tractor that has a bucket with teeth and overhead forks that clamp into the bale for moving.

Thirty-five years ago the haying process was much different. The hay was mowed as it is today. But only the dump rakes were utilized to create the wind rows. Car chassis equipment was used with wooden forks mounted on the front of the chassis and they would "sweep" down the wind rows collecting the hay onto the forks. These "sweeps" were then driven to the stack yard where the stacker was located. The loose hay was deposited onto the stacker's huge forks. Using another tractor, a cable was pulled which forced the arms of the stacker to rise into the air with the accumulated hay and much like a catapult, the hay was dumped into a three-sided cage made of boards and fencing where the hay stack was being built. Several "stackers"—usually two other individuals with pitch forks, moved the hay and packed it tightly within this cage, building the stack with each load. Eventually the sides of the hay stack reached the top of the cage and the hay stack sides were gradually brought in and packed until the stack was topped-off. The three sides of the cage were disassembled and set-up again to begin the process all over for another hay stack.

Today, before we feed hay to the cattle the hay wagons are loaded with one bale of hay. Hay is also shipped in to supplement the native hay grown here at the ranch. The shipped hay may consist of Alfalfa bales that can weigh over 1,600 pounds, or other types of hay—some of which are large square bales which can weigh over 1,500 pounds. Regardless of the type of hay, each bale is "broken" down by cutting the twine and then using pitchforks to separate the hay so that it can be "pitched" from a hay wagon using a truck to pull the wagon. This requires a driver for the truck and one person on the hay wagon pitching the hay into rows for feeding. Thirty-five years ago the loose hay was pitched into the hay wagons and then pitched again into rows in the same manner as today. The old hay wagons and dump rakes are still being utilized today for haying operations. The stacking cage, sweeps and stacker are long gone. Realistically, haying operations is much easier by yesterday's standards. But the seasons and weather for putting up hay and the feeding of hay are still the same—hot and cold.

THE LONG ROAD HOME

It takes awhile to get there—sometimes years … to travel that long road home. It's like me waiting for spring that comes only once a year. I've seen fifty-five of them arrive and transcend into summer. A damn long and sometimes hard road getting here. I find the soothing sound that good leather makes when you shift your weight in the saddle to be like an old melody that eases the souls of both horse and rider. A comforting feeling comparable to traveling that long road home. Spring time with thunder and lightening, warm winds and downpours. And green grass … all good stuff.

I went on line yesterday to http://www.cfdrodeo.com which is the website for Cheyenne Frontier Days. I decided to get a couple of tickets for Thursday July 29th so Michel and I could see Keith Urban and Trick Pony live in concert before there weren't any good seats left. I reserved seats in the center section where we can see and hear the music. A little something to look forward to—and it will give me a break from haying operations here at the ranch during that time. This year's Cheyenne Frontier Days runs from July 23rd to August 1st and has been in existence since 1897. I got my silver buckle at the 100th anniversary of Cheyenne Frontier Days back in 1996 and I will on occasions get that old buckle out of the box and look fondly upon that commemorative cowboy artifact. This year will be the 108th year for this event. And I can still vividly remember the 72nd Cheyenne Frontier Days.

I've always enjoyed rodeos, even when I was just a kid. One of my favorite events is the Wild Horse Race. That's where the rider, assisted by a mugger and a shank man must saddle a wild horse and ride once around the track in the proper direction to the finish line. There is a six minute time limit after the gun is fired. Last year there were forty-five teams competing with each team competing on three different days of the rodeo. The winning team is the one with the most money won.

There are other events but in my book the real cowboy artists are the ones who compete in the Wild Horse Race, Steer Roping, Team Roping and Calf Roping—all practical events of the present day. The audience really gets hyped-up over bull riding but I see no real advantage to riding a bull when there's a horse nearby. Bareback Riding and Saddle Bronc Riding are okay events too, but those events as well as Bull Riding are decided by judges making "judgmental" calls. With the Wild Horse Race, Steer Roping, Team Roping and Calf Roping you either cut the mustard or you don't—there's no real gray area or "personal" opinion interjected by some judgmental authority.

It's like while I'm attending Frontier Days and I'm eating at the various food stands and drinking a lot of beer—I'm either "plowed" or I'm not ... there's little in the way of "judgmental" decision making on my part. I'm there for a good time, and so are a lot of other folks. There are more cowboys and cowgirls here at the *Daddy of 'em All* than at any other time of the year. And it's the largest outdoor rodeo in the United States. The only thing that really hurts are the prices—that's why there are more people from Colorado in attendance than there are Wyomingites. Wyoming folks are poor—third lowest in the nation for personal income, while those from Colorado have money to burn. Here in Wyoming we have less people than any other state, including Alaska and Hawaii. We do have more Antelope than people though. That's a comforting fact. (Antelope make more sense to me than the majority of people.) And we have lots of cowboys and cowgirls as well. Guess that's why we're still called the Cowboy State.

Michel is not really into rodeos so I may have to attend some of the events without her. She was raised in the southwestern United States and speaks fluent Spanish, was a trainer of Thoroughbred horses that competed on the United States Olympic team, graduated from college with a degree in Zoology, is older and smarter than me, loves animals and is a wonderful little gal, so it's kind of hard for me to figure out why she doesn't care much for rodeos. She's more comfortable with the larger Thoroughbreds and her English saddle and tack instead of the smaller Quarter horse and western tack that I am accustomed to. Guess it's all about how one is raised. (As long as she has a hankering for this hell-bent-for-leather guy that's alright with me.) At least the two of us enjoy country music. So

I'll take her to the concert instead and hope she enjoys herself. There will always be … that long road home.

FALL RISING

There's a cold wind rising with the sun each morning now. Fall is unusually early for this time of the year. A few of the Cottonwood leaves sprinkle to the ground—leaves tinged with burnished edges. Young wildlife is in abundance—red foxes, porcupines, skunks, jackrabbits, badgers, mule deer and antelope seen scurrying during the early morning hours just before the sun crests the eastern horizon. I know what it's like to exist above the timber line in the mountains. I say, "exist" because one cannot live there year around, though the thought may entertain the non-experienced hiker. A mountain climate on the plains is not a regular occurrence here during the month of August at six-thousand feet above sea level. I'm getting older now, and when I consider that this farm boy from the Midwest has lived nearly half of his life on the high plains of Wyoming, certain signs in nature tell me a reoccurring story that I've read before. One need not search the clouds or look to a distant horizon for the next weather pattern moving in. The falling Cottonwood leaves don't necessarily tell a complete story either. The answer to the forecaster's quandary is beyond all weather patterns. It lies not in the sky above but on the ground below, and right at one's feet—ants.

Those little critters have been mighty busy throughout these summer months. I recently spent some time observing their activities, even chatting with a few of them during their travels back and forth from their duties. (It's hard holding a conversation with an ant.) I've never run across a lazy one that was still living, so when I do have the opportunity to carry on an occasional conversation with an ant the exchange is brief and to the point. (Ants don't observe any characteristics of the typical laid-back cowboy thought processes.) These little fellas basically tell me the same thing each time—*"Get out of my way. You're blocking traffic. Get somewhere!"* I move out of their way, and try again to engage in "small talk". The other day, one of these little guys took a break from work and leaned against a pebble to kind of look things over. I could tell by his presence that he was an old-timer. Looking up and seeing me, he paused briefly to contemplate my presence, then ask me what I was looking a(n)t. That was my cue that this particular gentleman was willing to engage in a conversation.

My first thought was to ask him what he thought about this year's upcoming elections, but then I quickly corrected myself when I realized that ants probably don't have a clue about politics. (Ants are more in tune with getting the work done at hand than talking about what they're going to do or have already accomplished.) Instead, I asked the old gentleman, "How's it going?" He looked up at me in a rather quizzed manner, scratched his chin with a foot and replied, *"I reckon it's about as good as it's going to get."* I could see right away that this was going to be a tough conversation. So I said, "Looks like you ants have been pretty darn busy this year from the looks of things here around the yard." He answered, *"What do you mean, young man?"* "Well, I see a lot of construction going on around here—ant hills being built and rerouted traffic all of the time," I replied. He gave me a wry smile and answered, *"This is Wyoming ain't it?"* I changed the subject, and instead asked him if he and the other ants were having any problems with the neighbors. *"What neighbors?"* He asked. "Well, you know … like people and pets, for example." He raised another leg and scratched behind his antenna with thoughtful contemplation. *"Naw, you folks and your pets don't bother us none. We do appreciate you setting out the occasional bowl of dog food, though I wonder how anyone can enjoy that stuff."* "Well, the dogs like it," I answer him. *"Humph!"* was his only answer. "You hear much from the other ant families around these parts?" I ask him. He was chewing on a blade of grass at the side of his mouth, stopped, then looked up at me, *"Why do you ask?"* "I just wanted to know if there's any news about what this winter is going to be like," I answered. The old ant replied, *"Yea, it's going to get cold this winter. Probably see some snow too."* "Humph!" was my answer. The old gent finally smiled and said, *"We think it's going to be a hard winter this year. Lots of snow and much colder than previous years here in these parts."* I asked him if he had seen many grasshoppers this year. He stated that most of the *Hoppies* (as he called them) had been too lazy during the previous year and had either died out or moved south to a warmer climate where they could lie around, drink booze and eat weed. (I figured the old gentleman didn't have too high a regard for the *Hoppies*.)

The old ant got back on his feet, stretched a bit then said—*"I got to get back to work. Time's a wastin' and I'm burnin' daylight. Don't worry about the weather. The weather will take care of its self. Nice talkin' with you young man."* I thanked him and watched, as he picked up something that weighed ten times what he weighed. He headed back into the mainstream of ant activity, leaving no doubt that he was quite capable of pulling his own weight. Everywhere I looked ants were working. Maybe I didn't need some Farmer's Almanac or a weather forecaster's predictions about what kind of winter it would be. With fall rising and all of the ants busy, I already had all the necessary prediction I needed.

Writer's Dilemma

A dear friend recently wrote me after I sent out my last article on *Horses and Weather;* Ron—*how would the United States defend itself if we had no government? Also, I just drove 1800 miles of public highway from* (omitted) *to Virginia Beach ... the mountains would be tough to cross without the Interstate Highway System. Personally, I am happy to pay my share of taxes for the good things that our government does for us. Iraq seems to me to be a place that needs some government ...*

Now there's some meaningful thought, and I truly appreciate that particular comment and the comments that I receive from others regarding my writings. I did write about some other things as well in that little piece, but what I write about and how I express my feelings affects different folks in different ways. People tend to concentrate on those things that stir them up. I know that when I send these articles out that I will most likely antagonize some people while reinforcing the opinions shared by others. It's kind of like getting a slap on the back and getting a kick in the ass ... all at the same time. It's what I call a writer's dilemma.

This is a great country. Where else would I be able to write without governmental interference? Ah ... but there is a problem. When the public reads a book regarding a controversial subject written by a controversial author liberty still rings. However, this is not always true regarding our news generated by the television networks and most of the newspapers. These forms of media are controlled by syndicates ... and the owners of the syndicates dictate what news stories will be broadcasted or printed, and how those stories will be manipulated to enhance either their own personal agenda or the government's position, whether true or false. I know that you may not believe this outright, but consider the "what if" should this actually be the scenario we are faced with regarding the disposition of our news stories—and then ask yourselves if what you have seen on television or read in the newspapers can be taken literally.

The war on terrorism invades our personal privacy. Some will explain that this is a necessary and minor loss of freedom when compared to the overall risks we are facing as a nation. I disagree, for I believe that freedom once lost is never regained. For example, a simple thing such as driving around the city streets of Cheyenne today I began keeping track of the cameras mounted above the various intersections throughout town. These cameras record the traffic, types of vehicles, who is driving what vehicle, their license plate numbers, time of day that they were at that particular intersection, which way they were heading, and so forth. If that doesn't bother you, then okay. But it bothers me because I want to know who is watching me and why? And what right do "they" have in keeping track of my whereabouts?

In the book, *Angels Don't Play This Harp*, Jeanne Manning and Dr. Nick Begich write about raising the roof of the world. *A four-year old child in his sandbox looks up at a blue sky with his eyes full of trust. His mother places a straw hat on his head, dabs sun blocking cream on his freckled nose, and expects that, because she shielded him from the sun's ultraviolet rays, he is safe from harmful radiation. But is he? Both his body and his planet are being penetrated by an unprecedented mix of man-caused radiations, and now the U.S. military plans to stir up the mix even further. They could go too far this time.* The book is about … *people who search for the truth about the Pentagon's project that is quietly being built at a remote outpost in Alaska. The $30 million project euphemistically named HAARP (High frequency Active Auroral Research Program) is made to beam more than 1.7 gigawatts (billion watts) of radiated power into the ionosphere—the electrically-charged layer above the Earth's atmosphere … After disturbing the ionosphere, the radiations will bounce back onto the earth in the form of long waves which penetrate our bodies, the ground and the oceans.* Even this cowboy can figure out that this affects everything we do here on the home range. Want to know more? Read the book … and then ask yourself which syndicated network or newspaper brought you the story. You guessed it … zip!

In the book, *Unequal Protection* written by Thom Hartmann, the author raises the question of how our country is controlled by corporations. *Was the Boston Tea Party the first WTO-style protest against transnational corporations? Did the Supreme Court sell out America's citizens in the nineteenth century, with consequences lasting to this day? Is there a way for American citizens to recover democracy of, by, and for the people?* The author begins by … *uncovering an original eyewitness account of the Boston Tea Party and demonstrates that it was provoked not by "taxation without representation" as it is commonly suggested but by the specific actions of the East India Company, which represented the commercial interests of the British elite.* Big Business and Big Brother are still at work today. You won't read it in the newspapers or see it on television, for obvious reasons.

I am not negative towards our country, but towards our government. It's not necessarily the differences of the present administration versus previous administrations that have held office in our congress, the presidency and the Supreme Court that I am concerned about—but the subtle erosion of individual liberty. So, in planning your next vacation, consider for a moment the information that can be readily gathered regarding you and your family. You've made preparations regarding your mail and newspaper deliveries. You may have notified your neighbor of your impending absence. The types of food you purchase using your local grocery's savings card or the medicines that you're taking by utilizing your pharmacy's card, all of your phone calls (including cellular) are recorded on computers—who you call, when you call, and how long you talked. Your cable or satellite provider monitors what programs you are watching. Those various magazine subscriptions tell others what your interests are or your political feelings. Your computer habits—such as who sends you email, who you send email to, what websites you visit ... all go through your provider's server. Your banking habits and credit card purchases not only are a record of what you purchased, but when you made the purchase, how much you spent, where you were at the time of purchase, and what you bought—all across this country. You leave town and those traffic intersection cameras takes their "Kodak moment" and then relays the information regarding your time and route of departure. At various locations throughout our interstate highways and the other cities you visit, your travel is monitored, the gas stations you stop at to refuel, the restaurants where you eat, the hotels you slept in, the souvenir shops in those quaint little out of the way places—all because you used a credit card, or wrote a check.

Your library card tells others the books you've checked out and are probably reading. The organizations that you are a member of and your voter's registration tell others your political intent. The OnStar system can locate you and your vehicle, if you've been in an accident or even unlock your doors for you—or others. The utility companies monitor your water, fuel and electrical usage. Did you hear about newborn babies having identity chips implanted in them without their parent's knowledge or permission? Or the government's subtle efforts in suppressing Michael Moore's forthcoming movie titled *Fahrenheit 911*. (If you've read Mr. Moore's book *Downsize This* you can understand the reasons why.) Every time you make a firearm purchase and fill out that required federal firearm form that everyone must now fill out—it tells our government the type of firearm, its caliber, its magazine capacity, your home address, your telephone number and your social security number and driver's license. Your government knows every legal gun owner's residence in this country.

If you'll be so kind as to give me your social security number, a driver's license or a credit card—I'll find you and your loved ones in the darkest of night. If I "hack" into your computer while you're online I'll find out even more about you and your family. But I don't, and I won't, because I respect your privacy and value my individual freedom and the freedom of others as well. If I desire to know more about those things that I am concerned about, my information won't necessarily come from television or the newspapers. Instead, I will seek publications and information written by others who are independent in their thought and who are not being paid by someone else to express those thoughts. And should you disagree or agree with what I write, it presently remains an individual liberty … and a writer's dilemma.

KELLY AND BUCKY

Kelly and Bucky are my companions during the nights when Michel is away at work. Both dogs are males … and so there is certain "bonding" that takes place while the Lady of this house is away—and a certain amount of mischief that we boys get into. Tonight, I took both Kelly and Bucky over to the bunkhouse to visit with Craig, who just happened to be taking a shower when we entered the front door. Both dogs were overly enthusiastic with this new environment and immediately set off to explore new sights and smells of the bunkhouse. Craig was not aware of our arrival, until I heard a loud shout emitted from his shower stall. (Kelly had proceeded to poke his head through the shower curtain to see what Craig was doing in there.) "Damn it Jordan, what the hell is going on!" were the words I received from the other end of the bunkhouse. Kelly ran back to me with a smile on his dog face … and the top of his head wet from Craig's shower. "Damn it Jordan … I'll get even with you!" It didn't matter by then—I was laughing so hard. Craig eventually showed up, chuckling about his recent "exposure". We each had a beer while we watched Bucky and Kelly further explore Craig's habitat. All of us boys were enjoying ourselves.

It doesn't take much to amuse Kelly, Bucky or me. We like to play together. We like to snack together. All of us like listening to country music. (Tonight we're listening to Suzy Bogguss greatest hits.) Later on we'll drink a little whisky and play a few hands of poker and afterwards we'll go outside and howl back at the coyotes. (There's nothing like stirring up the "neighborhood" late at night.) Kelly and Bucky do a better job of howling than I do … but I'll keep practicing anyway. And when we're all finally tuckered out we'll turn in for the night. It's a toss-up on who will get their favorite place on the floor … Kelly, Bucky or me. (We have to be rested up and sober before Michel gets back from work in the morning.) I haven't had a family to share life with for so long that it's refreshing to have companionship coming from three different sources all at once.

In a couple of months this fun will turn to hard work during the calving season. Long hours with little sleep, cold weather and blowing snow. We'll probably be short-handed and irritable. I won't see much of my family then and the time that I will have with each of them will be sporadic and brief. I hope they're willing to cope with me, as I love each of them.

This old cowboy knows a good life. The Lady of this home causes all of our tails to wag and it's a contest amongst us males seeking her attention. She has her hands full!

SIMPLE MECHANICS

"Mechanical" machinery remains more dependable than machinery powered by electricity, especially when mechanical machinery (such as windmills) is used in conjunction with nature. Reliable and crude in comparison with today's complex electrical systems, mechanical systems are relative repairable and serviceable. Electrical systems require either individual component replacement or total replacement. Without a source of power electrical systems will not operate. Today's society is dependent upon electricity. Nearly everything we utilize today has evolved from strictly mechanical operations to total electrical systems. All of this of course has the blessings of the fuel producing conglomerates such as the coal, petroleum and nuclear industries. Electricity enhances our lives, but makes us more dependable upon its usage. An item such as our old "mechanical" can opener that required little physical effort is replaced with an electric can opener. A garage door that previously opened by sliding the door to one side or swinging the door upwards is replaced with an electrical garage door opener. Gravity-flow or mechanical pumps requiring a little muscle power for fuel storage tanks have been replaced with electrical pumps for dispensing gas and diesel. The hand pump for that well water that brought forth drinking water has long been superceded with electrical pumps. In year's past those automobiles and trucks with simple mechanical fuel pumps, a coil and a set of points have been replaced by fuel-efficient and fuel-injected computerized vehicles that cost more than a home would have cost fifty years ago.

During my career in the United States Army I studied the resulting effects of thermonuclear explosions, in particular EMP (Electrical Magnetic Pulse). I found it rather interesting that if a nuclear bomb was detonated somewhere above in the earth's atmosphere its Electrical Magnetic Pulse would literally disrupt or destroy every transistorized/chip electrical system (including radio transmissions) within several hundred miles, dependent of course upon the size of the blast and its relative height above the earth's surface. This in essence would knock out every vehicle we drive or fly today, and that also includes our televisions, radios, computers, telephones, microwaves, clocks—anything in today's digital society. It would affect the fragile electrical components that make things work. Our communications would become nonexistent. (Things would be mighty quiet for awhile in the affected areas—a somewhat comforting thought). Those folks still driving around in those old vehicles with mechanical fuel pumps, a coil and a set of points would be waving to all of us "civilized" individuals sitting in our computerized vehicles along the road somewhere or stuck in the middle of our major metropolitan areas. "OnStar, are you there? Hello ... H E L L O!"

I am comfortable with mechanical machinery but I am very cautious of operating systems that are purely electrical. I don't totally trust electronics, mainly because I've encountered too many electronic failures in my lifetime. (I've received more "jolts" from electricity than I have "jabs" from mechanical things.) We tend to trust what we understand and distrust what we don't understand. Oh sure, I can wire things up and get the juice going where it should to go—but I still don't trust it. It's kind of like standing on top of a hill in the middle of a lightening storm—the more you play with it the more likelihood your chances of eventually getting struck.

Electricity has made our lives more comfortable—but at what price? Back in the fifties and sixties when we still had "tubes" in our radios and televisions (thermonuclear resistant) and our vehicles were primarily mechanical and not yet computerized, life was simpler (at least in my "mechanical" mind). We were frequently visited by unidentified flying objects (UFO's) whose occupants were fascinated by our mechanical civilization. Our planet was a museum for those visitors during that time period—a kind of "back to basics" in the mechanical sense. Those little fellas had a hankering for that particular time period, much like us historical buffs still enjoying the Old West. Our civilization has become more sophisticated and the little green guys don't come around anymore. Our high-tech society bores them. Those fellas were more interested in real cowboys than computerized suburbanites—I can't blame them for that.

Sitting on a buckboard wagon and driving a team of horses is more "romantic" to me than driving a SUV. You might not get there as quickly but the wagon has more interior space, better versatility in cross-country travel and the "pollution" that the team of horses creates is greatly appreciated by Mother Nature—purely mechanical, and for a lower price. Of course it's not really practical by today's standards. Our "get-up-and-go" has "got-up-and-went". So we demand comfort and convenience in our vehicles and appliances with all of those bells and whistles.

The going price for a "Plain-Jane" cow pony nowadays is pretty reasonable. For five or six-hundred bucks you get all of the amenities such as four-wheel drive, air conditioning, and cruise control. Buy a few accessories in the way of saddle and tack and you get a great seat, a nice blanket, a frog or some lace (your preference), fenders, a skirt, a horn—you even get great rear housing. No electronics and a means of travel that will love you as well as you love it. You can take that to the bank!

MARRIAGE AND ACHES

This winter weather takes its toll on me. I must be getting older ... because I sure as hell don't feel any younger. I have aches where I didn't know that I was supposed to have "feeling". Lately it has been back "aches" that have reminded me of my vulnerability to heavy lifting and twisting. This week we sent one of the ATV's in for repair of a cracked frame and new front struts. The other ATV has not run for the last couple of days—an electrical problem that I can't seem to find. (No "spark" to the spark plug.) It's been driving me nuts. We use the ATV's to bring the steers in for cake feeding in the morning. By three o'clock this afternoon my patience had reached its limit and I packed-up my tools and called it quits for the day on this particular ATV. I was losing my "perspective" and objectivity in diagnosing the problem. I told Rod that I was bringing in a horse for tomorrow's roundup of the steers. He asked me if a horse was more reliable than a machine. (I know Rod ... he doesn't like ATV's.) I replied, "Damn right! I don't have to worry about a horse not starting." So, in the morning I'll have aches of another type.

Then there are the mental "aches". I haven't had a vacation since the mid nineties. I figure that I am overdue. I have had "time off" for brief periods but not a vacation. I reckon that affects a person's outlook on a lot of things. Michel comes home from work so tired in the mornings and then I go to bed at night feeling the same way. You'd think that two people working hard all of their lives would get a break from it all somewhere down the line. We share our "aches" with one another. I would like to grow old gracefully. Lately, I haven't found "graceful" in anything I've done. I put pain on the back burner and worry about it later. One of these days it's going to catch up with me. Now I know why they invented drugs, alcohol and marriage ... escape tools to get away from reality. Michel tells me that if I continue to pursue the marriage thing that she she's going to run. (She enjoys "reality" more than I do.) So I'm not making any headway on a date for marriage. But that's okay for now … as long as we have each other.

I got to thinking about what constitutes a "marriage". I know a lot of couples who are not married that get along with one another better than a husband and a wife. Maybe marriage is society's stamp of approval. Maybe it's okay then to "ache". I brought up the subject of marriage and the concept of a western wedding a couple of days ago. Michel's response was more in line of utilizing a Justice of the Peace instead. I tend to agree with her … just get it over with so I can get to bed on time and get my rest. We can have our honeymoon when we're in our eighties and share the same cup for our dentures. Romantic! That's what she calls me … romantic. By then I'll be so busted-up that once I do get into bed I'll never be able to get up again.

Love aches. Like a toothache, I have certain fondness for sweets. Guess that's why I want to marry Michel … that fondness for sweetness. (I'll worry about the tooth ache thing later.) I figure that life is too short to piddle around. I've missed out on a lot of things in my life. But the "aches" are constant reminders of what I haven't missed out on. Reassurances of reality.

TELEPHONE SERVICE

My new telephone service will be with RT Communications. I have been trying to get my own phone line activated since the 4th of December. But things are different out here at the ranch. The first phone service here at the ranch was not established until 1963 (the ranch was founded in 1889). The building I maintain here at the ranch had a phone line installed around 1983 but has not been used since that time. Currently the phone line is activated but is the same line as Barbie's phone (Rod Kirkbride's daughter). Most of us readily accept the convenience of modern day technology and the speed in which our phones can be activated. Not so here in this part of Wyoming.

Before RT Communications of Wheatland, Wyoming could provide service they wanted to know if I had previous telephone service. "Sure—Qwest, AT&T, Bell … you name it," I replied. They responded that was fine but they needed a Letter of Credit from my previous phone company. They said I could fax it to them. I called Qwest and requested that they fax the Letter of Credit to RT Communications. Nope—Qwest won't fax anything to RT Communications. Qwest said they had to mail it to me instead. They sent the mail out somewhere around the 5th of December and I received the Letter of Credit on the 12th of December and faxed it to RT Communications. They scheduled service for the 22nd of December or sooner. (It will now be the 22nd.)

Meanwhile, "back at the ranch" RT Communications called and wanted to know what the building number was for the installation. So I'm thinking, "Building number! You guys must be nuts! There's a multitude of buildings scattered over the twenty-one thousand acres here at this part of the ranch." (They needed a building number for 911 purposes.) Now I got to tell you folks that if I ever need the services of 911 I sure as hell won't be anywhere near a phone to make that call. I'll get taken out by a mad bull, thrown from a horse or smashed-up in the corrals—none of which are anywhere near my phone! Anyway, The Laramie County Engineers had to determine what the building number was. This they have finally accomplished. And now that this building has a number I'm suppose to have my own telephone number and service on the 22nd of this month. But I'm not holding my breath. Another weather front could roll through this region and prolong that possibility again. (It's impossible to shovel out fifteen miles of driveway!"

So folks, there you have it. Modern technology at its best. Somehow I have difficulty absorbing this on a cold winter day with the wind howling at sixty mph and waiting for a telephone guy to show up in his heated truck. I guess I'd be better off just to kiss one of the bulls and have a shot of whisky on the side!

OLD TIMES

Sage brush and the short-stemmed new grass intermixed with the golden strands of the older and longer grasses of last year. Prickly pear cacti poke out amongst the rocky outcrops along the rough truck path and we pass by an old rock watering tank where a windmill stood years ago. Rod is driving his Toyota truck, I'm in the passenger seat and Craig is in the truck's bed. We're heading back to the ranch buildings still several miles away. Yesterday we had to pull two sections of pipe at one of the windmills because the rod had broken into inside the pipe. We had to replace the rod to get this one windmill back into operation before the cattle are moved onto this particular range on Saturday.

This morning after the feeding was accomplished; we herded some of the mothers and their calves into the corrals and separated the calves out for branding. I rode Foxy who didn't like the noise from the John Deere Gator that Craig was driving. Foxy started crow-hopping (bucking with little effort) as I tried to settle her down. We got the calves separated and began the branding operation utilizing the new branding chute for the first time. This new contraption works real well and doesn't appear to cause as much stress to the calf as the old method of "throwing" one to the ground. (I've enclosed a couple of photos of the new branding process with this correspondence.) Rod began the branding and I traded places with him later on. We branded sixty-eight calves today. Barbie did the cutting and pasting, Gabe turned the chute and held the hind legs of the calves, Katrina gave the calves their shots, Rod and I branded, and Craig and Justin were in the holding pen battling the calves into position and running them into the chute (rough work). David took care of the head part of the chute. When it was all over, only one calf had escaped through the new chute and we took care of this one calf on the ground using the old "throw" method—for old time's sake. Tomorrow we'll brand some more.

Yesterday, after the one windmill had been repaired, I asked Rod how long he figured those old pump rods had been in that pipe. He said that most of those rods have been in there working away since the 1930's; maybe the early forties. This August after the cattle are moved out of that particular range, we'll pull everything out of the ground and put in new pipe (about six sections) and new pump rods and "leathers"—basically rebuilding this windmill. I figure that's not too bad, considering that in today's "modern" age most computers are out of date by the time the newer models come out the following year.

On the outskirts north of Cheyenne one can see a new home being built every week—sometimes a couple of homes are being constructed at the same time. Each home is anywhere from a quarter-million to over half-million in price and sits on several acres of land—that was good grazing land when I was a youngster here thirty-six years ago. Cheyenne is expanding ... without its heritage. Too many out-of-state people are moving here to this southeastern portion of Wyoming. The metropolitan area keeps edging its way towards the ranch. "Modernization" marches onward and the old, well the old ... just passes away.

Riding along that old path today with Rod and passing that old stone watering tank belonging to a long-departed homesteader got me to thinking. "Rod, how many folks do you reckon were living around these parts about seventy years ago?" I asked. He told me that probably one household for every half section of land. And now they're coming back again.

Back in the 1890's it took the Kirkbrides a couple of days by horse and wagon to reach Cheyenne, pick up supplies, and get back to the ranch again. Today, I can drive to Cheyenne in about forty-five minutes. In the not too distant future ... Cheyenne will be here instead. Hopefully, I won't be around then to worry about driving anywhere.

SELF-SUFFICIENT

The Cattail Ranch is self-sufficient in many ways. There's no shortage of "beef" for instance. (That television advertisement that played several years ago of "Where's the beef?" has no relevance here.) Just take a look and you'll see it hoofing along. We have two types of telephones here in our home—the cordless phone is used for most calls. The other phone is a slim line model that sits here beside the computer and is used in the event the power goes out. (Cordless phones require electricity to work—no electricity, no phone.) Our heat is provided by propane fuel tanks for all of the ranch homes, which also include a heated water tank for the steers. All of the ranch homes have propane water heaters as well. No electricity, no problem. All of the cooking stoves are also propane. Each ranch home has a satellite dish(s) for television (Dish TV). No electricity … well of course, no TV. (One can't have everything when the power goes out.) Water for all of our homes is provided by windmill and the water is stored in an underground cistern on top of the hill north of the ranch buildings. Water is gravity-fed and so if there's no electricity we still have water, even toilet facilities. Water for all of the corrals and outlying water tanks at the various ranges is provided by windmills. Some of these also have underground cisterns while some have holding tanks above ground level.

A couple of weeks ago a neighboring rancher and friend requested our help because his windmill quit pumping. He had cattle that needed water and fortunately the weather was warmer, which provided some snow-melt during the couple of days his windmill was down. The pump rod had broken at the top of the mill just below the "motor". The fan blades were still turning but of course no water was being pumped. I climbed to the top of the tower and assisted the others on the ground in pulling the pipe sections from the well. Each section is approximately twenty-one feet of inch-and-a-quarter galvanized pipe enclosing the same length of a pump rod section that is coupled to other pump rod sections with a threaded coupling inside the pipe. Needless to say, it takes quite a bit of effort in "pulling" a well, depending upon the depth of the well. We ended up rebuilding this particular windmill by replacing all of the sections with new pipe. We also reconfigured the pipe outlet to the water tank. I inspected the gears in the motor on top of the mill and refilled the gear box with oil. Standing atop of a small and oily platform thirty feet or more off the ground without any safety equipment and with the wind blowing and trying to hold onto tools with one hand and maintaining a grip on the oily structure with my other hand does raise the "pucker factor" a tad. But we got the job done and our neighbor now has plenty of water.

Putting the technical data aside, a windmill sits over a drilled well hole. The pipe runs to the bottom of the well hole. At the bottom of the pipe are slits or holes that allow the water to enter the pipe. The pump rod that runs through the center of the pipe and "leathers" or plungers on the well end of the pipe provides suction to draw the water up through the pipe. The pumping action is provided by the fans atop the tower. The fans are mounted to a housing that contains the gears. A "tail" is mounted to the housing so that when the wind blows it catches the tail and swings the fan blades so that they are facing into the wind. As the fans turn they in turn rotate the gears inside the housing or "motor" causing the pump rod to rise and fall inside the pipe—thus the suction to the water in the bottom of the well hole. The water is pulled up inside the pipe to the surface where is allowed to flow into another pipe that takes the water to the water tank or underground cistern. The windmill can be turned off by applying a "brake" to the fan housing. Basically, a wire is attached to an arm at one corner of the tower at ground level. The wire reaches to the top of the tower where it is attached to a metal arm so that when pressure is applied to the arm at ground level by pulling the arm downward this same wire pulls the metal arm atop the tower. This pulls the "tail" inward so that the fans no longer face the wind and at the same time causes the brake hub to engage, thus stopping the fans from turning with the wind. To turn the windmill on again one just has to release the arm at ground level once more. Simple—when everything is working properly. Still … it's a lot cheaper than electricity, electric pumps and electrical power lines out to the middle of nowhere. But it can be a lot of work when things get broken.

We have around twenty-one windmills scattered around the ranch and outlying areas. Most are turned off in the winter. Those that are kept running require breaking ice in the tanks. Cold temperatures can cause the ice to thicken to six inches or more in one night. Cattle have to drink of course. And there's your short course in Windmills 101. Now get up there and keep those windmills going and the water flowing!

SMILES

Colder weather is on the way for this weekend with the possibility of some snow again. Winter's routine here at the ranch. Up at five in the morning. Dress and shave, turn on the coffee pot, make the bed and put on my work boots and cold weather clothing, drink some coffee, then out the door by five-forty and over to the bunkhouse where Craig and I share some conversation and more coffee before heading out the bunkhouse door and over to the barn and corrals for the morning chores. Back again to my home by six-twenty a.m. where I sit and hope for a pink-hued sunrise until they call me on the PA system for breakfast, which is usually sometime between six-fifty to seven-ten a.m. Breakfast conversation with Craig, Barbie, Rod and Mae and then it's back to my home to get warmly dressed again for the morning's feeding. Craig goes out on the ATV and brings the steers to the gates of the corrals. In the meantime I'm cleaning the feed troughs of snow and pouring out cake for the steers. Barbie and I open the gates and the steers come charging through. One really has to know cattle to detect a "smile" on a steer's face. But I know a smile and a good breakfast when I see one. Next, it's out to the hay wagons. Rod pulls one wagon with his truck with Craig pitching hay; Barbie pulls the other wagon with her truck and me pitching hay. Back to the corrals and the steers are let out to stampede to the hay. More smiles on furry faces.

I load Barbie's truck with cake for the heifers and she takes off to pick-up Mike, her husband, and they head off to the creek to the east. Sometimes I go with Barbie and give Mike a break. At the creek we gather up the heifers and cake them on the ground. If the snow is deep we hook a snow plow on the back of the truck and make swaths through the snow before we put out the cake. Heifers smile too when they get their cake. While they're eating we drive to the stack yard and break down a round bale of hay. When the heifers are done with their cake I climb on the hay wagon and pitch the whole wagon while Barbie drives the truck. Back to the stack yard and we put the next day's bale on the wagon then hook-up the "dune buggy" which has alfalfa hay on it. Back to the heifers where I pitch more hay. More smiles. Drop off the dune buggy in the stack yard and back to the ranch.

If I don't go with Barbie to feed the heifers then I'll usually go with Craig to feed the bulls in the opposite direction—to the west. We load up cake bags and fill the truck with hay. We stop by to bust the ice out of the horses' water tank. Off we go in pursuit of these twenty-five monstrous brutes. Once found, it becomes a race of getting the cake poured upon the ground and out of the way before fifteen-hundred pounds of muscle slams you into eternity. Then we pitch hay to these fellows as well. I don't know if bulls "smile" or not—and I really don't give a damn by that point in time. We stop by their water tank and bust the ice in there, if required. We drive back to the ranch, break down the hay bales on the wagons for the next morning's feeding; refill the cake buckets and sacks. By now, it's ten or ten-thirty in the morning and we're ready to go to work.

What the day's work will consist of is a toss-up. Our agenda is basically driven by Rod and what he wants to accomplish that day. Presently we've been working on building up another stock truck—that will give us three trucks to haul cattle in. I'm welding and grinding away. Sometime I have to repair whatever vehicle or piece of equipment that goes down. So far I've replaced a starter in one of the Toyota trucks, replaced the starter in a stock truck, replaced the exhaust system on another Toyota, a battery and the fuel pump relay in the F-350 Ford, changed the oil and filter and greased the hay-loading tractor, tested all of the vehicles' antifreeze condition (that's about twenty-five trucks, tractors and cars), repaired the fuel regulator on the bunkhouse stove and stopped a propane leak in the bunkhouse so that Craig had heat and wouldn't blow himself to hell and back again. I've repaired some barbed wire fencing that the steers were working on in gaining some additional freedom. The heifers will have to be trail-driven back to the ranch soon for their vaccinations and herded back east again. But any given day could be something different in the way of work after the morning feeding is done. Sometime around noon is dinner, and time to get warm.

Then there is the weather. My hands have hurt so badly in the cold that I have a tough time just grasping something for any length of time. My finger tips split and bleed. My feet have gone numb and my face has been chapped from the wind and cold so much so that it burns when I do get back into a heated building. Ah yes ... they call that a "ruddy" complexion. No smiles there folks. Finally, around four-thirty in the afternoon it's back to the corrals for the evening's chores. That done, I head back to my home. It's dark now again ... just like it was for the morning's chores. I rest until they page me for supper. If it's laundry night for me I'll start it before supper. I carry my laundry basket over to the milk room where the washer and dryer are located. (Oh yes, I had to repair the dryer's latch as well as replace the hot water faucet in the milk room and replace the kitchen faucet on Barbie's sink, and all of the copper plumbing under the sink where there were three good leaks.) I try to get some reading done in the evenings, some emails answered, and more recently—get back into my writing mode.

I have three great moments in my day where it is my turn to smile. The first one is in the early morning hours when Michel calls me when she gets off of work. I call that my "wake-up call". It's a wonderful way to start my day! The second great moment comes at the end of my day when Michel calls me before she heads off to work again for the night shift. That call sets my mind to writing. And

I smile again. I don't have much time off from the winter's routine here at the ranch. What little time I have off is after feeding on Sunday mornings until later in the day when it's time to do chores again. I try to get into Cheyenne sometime during the week to get some items for Craig and myself. I'll leave for town forty miles away to see Michel or make myself available here at the ranch for her when we can spend a little time together—which isn't often enough for this old boy.

I suppose that there is some cowboy glamour somewhere in all of this that I do on a daily basis. I don't gain weight because I never slow down, though I can eat like a horse. But the work and cold weather takes it all out of me. By nine-thirty at night I'm ready for a hot shower and by ten o'clock I'm about wound down for the day. I know that five o'clock will come early enough. As I close my eyes, I say my prayers … my third great moment of the day … and I smile.

SOMEWHERE

I went out towards the corrals the other day and found Rod sitting in his truck by the main gate. I asked him where everyone was. He laughed and replied that the old man had once told him a story about this fella coming home to find his wife naked in bed and a pair of bare feet sticking out from underneath the bed. The man yelled at this fella under his bed and asked him what he was doing under there. This fella replied, "Well … every son-of-bitch has to be somewhere." I guess that pretty well answered my question regarding the whereabouts of the others.

These last few days have kept me busy attending to various tasks involving ranch life. I worked on two stock trucks that had lighting problems—replacing light bulbs, repairing the broken wiring and replacing the flashers. Now, all of the lights work again. I also replaced the spark plug in the motor for the cement mixer. Yesterday I was up on three windmills doing regular maintenance and then I was on horseback helping Rod and the others sort out some dry cows for market. I rode Raggy and afterwards I gave her a sweaty workout out in the meadow. (Actually, she gave me the workout.) Raggy tossed Craig out of the saddle some time back when she was going full tilt and busted Craig up pretty good. He still feels the effects. I owed Raggy one for Craig.

I got the other ATV running today and with Craig on the other ATV we moved the horses back to the Gusher. I forgot that I didn't have much in the way of brakes on my ATV and nearly catapulted myself over a hillside drop-off when I almost didn't stop soon enough. The other day I helped in branding one of the bulls whose name is Winston. Actually, all I did was hold the rope tight around his horns. Rod did the branding and Barbie passed the irons. Winston didn't care to have the T-Quarter-Circle planted on his hide and tried a couple of times to climb out of the chute. But he is "marked" now, and in better spirits.

I replaced a couple windshield wipers on two trucks this morning. It's colder now and with the light snow a bad wiper makes for bad vision. I also replaced the seats in our kitchen water faucets, disassembled and cleaned out the shower head in the bathroom, and removed all of the caked-up lime deposits around the faucet fixture in the bathroom sink. Easy stuff—and a lot safer. We did get the new branding chute set up the other day. Looks like we'll schedule the branding of the calves next week on Wednesday, May 5th. This will be a "First" here at the Cattail Ranch. It has always been done the old way before. I hope to get some pictures of this new contraption in progress. Of course, we'll continue to utilize the fire pit for heating the branding irons. One shouldn't jump too quickly into the future or you might lose touch with reality. After all, that's what living on this ranch in Wyoming is all about—*reality.*

Tomorrow, it's back to work at Lowe's again. Michel went back to work there today and she wasn't looking forward to it at all. Too many people and too much noise for the two of us. But, "every son-of-a-bitch has to be somewhere"—though I'd rather be here at the ranch. I don't know how you folks like spending your "time off" but for me my time off is here. Sometimes when I do go into town … I feel like a domesticated cow turd.

THE VILLAIN

"There's the villain!" I'm in the shop getting ready to put the air compressor away when I hear Mae's voice outside. *Villain? What the hell did I do now?*, I wonder to myself. "Hi Mae! So I'm a villain now—what did I do to become a villain?" "You killed a rattlesnake! Why did you kill that rattlesnake?" *Oh oh … I'm in deep doo-doo now!* "Because he was in my way," I replied. "He wasn't in your way—he was on the road! You know, one of these days the rattlesnake will be an extinct species because everyone keeps killing them." *Well, I've lost this war before it even got started—and I didn't even have a chance to get ready.* We change the subject from rattlesnakes to politics and John Kerry instead. Politics aren't that much safer, but at least we can find a subject on more common ground, such as the environment, to talk about.

Bush doesn't have an environmental policy. As a matter of fact, Bush will most likely go down in history as the worst president regarding the environment. But it wasn't always that way. In this month's *Sierra* magazine there's an article titled: *The Green Old Party*. The article goes on to explain that the GOP used to be staunch conservationists. Theodore Roosevelt led the way of course. He established the U.S. Forest Service, created five national parks, designated 51 bird reserves and 4 game preserves, and proclaimed 18 national monuments. Dwight Eisenhower set aside 8.9 million acres in northeastern Alaska that is now part of the Artic National Wildlife Refuge—the same area that Bush wants corporations to drill for oil in. Richard Nixon signed into law The Clean Air Act, the National Environmental Policy Act, the Environmental Pesticide Control Act, and the Endangered Species Act. He also established the Environmental Protection Agency and brought in environmental leaders to run it. Now, there's movement a foot to get the Republican Party back where it should be regarding the environment. That will only happen when Oil-Slick Georgie is history.

John Kerry is pro-environment. He's also for the working stiff instead of the big corporations. He gets my vote there because I enjoy clean air and water and unsoiled wilderness areas. I also *work for a living* because I have to eat and pay my bills, and I don't have any stockholders to bother me about their million dollar homes or the fact that their Mercedes or Hummer doesn't hold enough groceries when they go shopping. I am leery of Mr. Kerry's stance on firearms control though. I do not want to see the reemergence of the "Brady Bunch" in Washington! But if we don't have clean air and water I won't have any need to worry about gun control—Oil Slick Georgie will do that for me without firing a shot. I have no fondness for the Bush administration. He may not have dodged the draft but he sure dodged the Viet Nam War. He later crowed like a rooster on the deck of that aircraft carrier when he announced that the conflict in Iraq was over. Yea … right! Mr. Kerry didn't dodge the war in Viet Nam nor did he try to hide his feelings when he spoke out as a veteran against what our country was doing in Viet Nam. So as a "real" veteran, he gets my vote there too.

As for the rest of the political amphitheater, it remains a wait-and-see scenario for me. I'll probably vote for John Kerry because the only other choice is no choice at all. As for myself and the *Villain* character that I've become, I've decided that Mae just might be right about protecting those rattlesnakes. So, I've decided to carry a cooler and a long forked-stick in my truck from now on. That way when I find one of those endangered rattlesnakes I can capture it and put it in the cooler and then transport it to a safer habitat … like Mae's back yard.

THE SHORTEST DAY

Shortest day of the year today, and the longest of nights. Christmas arrives in a few days and the daylight hours will be increasing by then. It doesn't matter though, because both are imperceptible measurements. How does one "measure" light or an event that occurred centuries ago? Here at the ranch away from the hustle and bustle of city life and people interacting with people, I have more time to think without worrying about what others want me to think.

I had the opportunity to leave the ranch for a few hours yesterday so I took the red pony into Cheyenne to get a few things that I needed. (I had not been in town since the 4th of December.) Leaving the ranch for the drive into town, I felt total freedom as the sun began to set in the west. I accelerated and concentrated on my driving while shifted through the various gears as I traveled the gravel road at seventy mph. I went completely sideways a couple of times in the curves as I steered the opposite direction trying to keep that Cayuse of mine going where I wanted it to go. I arrived safely in town and found that nothing had changed except that I no longer lived there—I didn't miss my absence, nor do I think anyone who lived in Cheyenne notice that I wasn't around anymore.

The drive back on those fifteen miles of gravel road wasn't much different than the trip into town. I didn't give a damn if I rolled that pony of mine or not. I figured that eventually someone would find me, or what was left of me, and it would probably be in the blotter and later on the obituary page that I had gone airborne—leaving the road going in excess of seventy mph doing cartwheels and eventually coming to a rest in some gulch or on top of some rock pile out in the middle of nowhere. Maybe what I need is rest. Sometimes just trying to figure people out and doing what "society" expects of me is too much to attempt.

I attempted to make several telephone calls today. I wanted to talk with my daughter and my son, but neither answered their phones. I tried calling a couple of friends before they headed into work tonight with the same results. I also tried calling that sweetheart of mine, but got no answer. So the ones that matter the most to me and that I really wanted to share a little time with on the phone weren't available. Not being "available" seems to be my life's story. I have been categorized by some folks as being somewhat impetuous or always wanting to get things quickly accomplished. Perhaps I am. But I know what it is to seize the moment … or to lose that one opportunity that comes only once in a lifetime. And a "lifetime" is all we have … and some are shorter than others.

It's not death that I fear. Rather I fear not living life instead—that, and the pain or suffering that I could possibly cause to others. *Give me time* … but I can't do that. I can't give "time" to someone else, because I don't have it to give. We either take the time given us at the moment it is presented, or wish we had done so at some later date.

I have been invited on Christmas day to spend some time with some dear friends in Cheyenne. I said that I would do so. Now I'm not so sure that taking that trip into town would do me any good, or that my presence in Cheyenne would make any difference. Riding a horse that is trying to put me into the ground or a bull that is trying to kill both of us just angers me. I've "tempered" my anger over the years and that worries me. Maybe I've loss something worthwhile in my life. I'd rather feel anger than have no feeling at all. I'd rather live today and let tomorrow take its course.

THE WHOLE PICTURE

I received my new roping saddle this week. I put my saddle on Foxy, who was skittish with all of the "creaking" noise that new leather makes. We moved some heifers from the Pence range today over to the Sterling. The two bulls that were in with the heifers were loaded up and trucked back to the corrals, where they were corralled with two other bulls With four riders we moved the four bulls north to the Round Hill. The only thing the bulls had on their mind was fighting. The number ninety bull has been especially aggressive and wasn't the least bit concerned about taking anyone out. But with Barbie riding Lucy and her dog Bluebell snapping at the bulls heels, Jake riding Trigger, and Adrian (who is a French citizen visiting the ranch this summer) riding Charles, we got the bulls moved. No mishaps in our little excursion. I enjoyed riding my new saddle, even though Foxy is old and cantankerous and has about as much get-up-and-go as I do when I get up at four o'clock in the morning.

I did a little mechanical work today as well. I replaced the master cylinder on one of the trucks and bled the brake lines, then repaired the wiper fluid hose connection under the cowling on Mae's car. Tomorrow Michel and I return to Lowe's Regional Distribution Center for our three-day work week again. At least we only have to work half a day (six hours) on Sunday, July the Fourth. Michel's son (Tim) and his lady (Mickey) will be here at the ranch to visit Monday. My daughter Amanda will also be arriving Monday as well. I'll meet her in Cheyenne at nine o'clock in the morning and she'll follow me back to the ranch so she won't get lost (cell phones only work in a couple of areas north of town and the rest of the areas are "dead" zones with no signal). I haven't seen Amanda since last

October and she wants to get away from city life in Denver for a day because she says it's driving her crazy. (Imagine that—city life driving somebody crazy!) I told her to come on out for a little rest and relaxation, breathe some clean air, and stomp in some cow shit for a change of pace. We might ride some horses—she can ride Foxy. That way the two "burnt-out" ones can be together.

We received a good amount of much-needed moisture in the month of June here at the ranch. The vegetation has greened-up considerably and the native grass is doing well so far. If we don't get any severe hail storms that beat the hay crop into the ground we just might have a good cutting of hay later this month. Out riding today I saw another rattlesnake, which was a good size one. That's the third one I've seen so far this year. I don't like rattlers—they're sneaky and they can do some serious tissue damage if they don't kill you first. If you get to the hospital in Cheyenne within two hours after you're bitten the folks there can shoot you full of anti-venom medicine. That might be difficult if you're bitten and you're out riding miles from the main ranch. I'd just as soon shoot the rattler than have someone shoot me. Back when I was a tadpole and growing up on the farm back in Indiana we would occasionally get a huge snapping turtle in the farm yard. Folk lore had it that if a snapping turtle got a hold of you he wouldn't let go until it thundered. I told one of the farmers up the road that story and he replied, "By God … if a big snapper got a hold of me it's going to thunder!" I believed him too.

Actually, rattlesnakes are a part of all God's creatures. I've seen a lot of wildlife around the ranch here this spring—wild turkeys, antelope and mule deer with tiny fawns, hawks and eagles, beaver down at the creek, badgers, coyotes, skunks, and of course those damn rattlers. I reckon you have to take the good with the bad to get the whole picture. Getting the whole picture can't be done with a camera. Pictures don't breath or smell and they don't make noise. You can't "feel" what's in a picture and nothing moves in a picture. Pictures stop time forever. Sometimes that's good—a moment in history. But I'd rather see the moment go on … and live that moment forever.

STEERS AND QUEERS

I returned to work at Lowe's last Friday. (My beer supply was getting low.) Actually, I had previously requested a three-month leave of absence, which took management by surprise because I had not given them any advance notice. (They explained that to me when I returned to work.) So, I continued to unload the same semi-trailer of porcelain sinks and pedestals by myself Saturday afternoon and again Sunday morning, and I almost had it all done. But by late Sunday morning, with the temperature rising inside that trailer and the constant inhaling of the porcelain dust from the boxes I was unloading, I was getting damn tired. Mentally, I decided that I was not going to volunteer for overtime on Monday. Physically, I figured that I wasn't even going to make it through the rest of the day. A couple of more hours went by of the S.O.S. (acronym for same old shit). I decided that this job just wasn't worth it. I staggered out of the semi-trailer knocking the dust from my clothing, climbed on my forklift, and drove to the front office. I stopped just long enough to clean my personal items out of my locker, walked to the front office and handed the company items and my identification badge to the administrative assistant sitting at the front counter and said, *"I'm out of here!"* She looked at me with mouth opened—but never said a word. (And I wasn't even "packing".) So ended my illustrious career at Lowe's. I guess they'll have to find another college-educated idiot to take my place.

Other than the job itself, other irritations were constantly present. (I know that some people may think I'm being "petty" about some of these bothersome irritations but I'll go ahead and explain my feelings anyway.) To begin with, I was tired of continually observing all of the employee tattoos. (The "females" wore more tattoos than the males.) There were tattoos on the neck, the arms, the legs, and the ankles (and probably other regions that I didn't want to even to think about). Most tattoos were of poor quality and signified nothing less than slob "art" in my opinion. My reasoning was that the individual must have been drunk when this "art" work was performed—if not, they sure would have gotten drunk thereafter. Another major irritation was the number of lesbians and their social clique there at Lowe's. I really don't care about an individual's sexual preference—except when it directly impacts the work at hand. When a company such as Lowe's has two members of management that are lesbians sharing the same home and sleeping together they often overlook the behavior and work ethics of other "females" with similar persuasions. If any of the males were gay they certainly didn't display any tendencies that I could observe. And few of the males were tattooed to the extent that the "female" billboards were tattooed. Okay—I apologize for not utilizing the right terminology regarding the gay community, but I have my rights too and I'd rather distance myself from these social retards. I agree that a little tattoo art goes a long way and can actually accentuate some body regions—like tattooing the ears of cattle for example.

Body piercing was just as prevalent as tattoos at Lowe's. The "males" that wore an earring did so in a conservative manner. (I never could figure out that right-ear versus left-ear stuff—I figure that any male who wears an earring is a bit on the prissy side regardless.) Bullet, bayonet and shrapnel scars are more beautiful to me than tattoos and they tell a more complete story—here stands a man instead of some artistic flower-child want-to-be man. Okay, so I'm not into the latest trends. But wearing an earring in the nose, bottom lip, tongue, eyebrow or naval just doesn't do anything for me. (We use to ring the hogs' nose back on the farm and an occasional bull here at the ranch, but not for artwork.) My daughter told me that she saw a couple (I presume it was a male and female) that were dressed alike walking down the sidewalk in Denver. The "male" had a collar around his neck with a leash that the "female" was holding on to. I reckon there are elements in our society who would consider this as a "romantic" jester. I think that the female in this scenario was more of a man and the man was more of a female. But who am I to judge? Anyway, enough about the dykes and dicks at Lowe's

Another irritant was the water quality. Lowe's policy was that water was the only form of liquid allowed in the warehouse, and it had to be in a clear plastic container. (I had thoughts about substituting gin or vodka in my water bottle on a bad workday.) A couple of swigs of Lowe's water and your stomach started gurgling within minutes. (Swamp water would have been more nutritious.) It didn't matter that you might be working yourself to death and that your body required a couple of gallons of water a day just to replenish what you sweated out—Lowe's was considerate enough to provide free water, if you could stomach it. That, and a fifteen minute break after three steady hours of work, a half-hour lunch break after another three hours of work, and one more fifteen-minute break at the end of another three hours of work before you ended a twelve-hour workday three hours after that. Now that's my kind of recovery! It didn't matter if you were lifting one-hundred pound boxes all day or pushing a pencil—everyone got the same breaks. The only thing was, those in management never lent a hand to those doing the physical work in order to acquire a better understanding of what the individual was actually going through. *"Make sure you drink some water!"*

This particular warehouse has the worst safety record of any warehouse in the Lowe's system. Back injuries are number one—go figure! Accidents due to improper use of equipment are right up there too. We've had accidents that required amputations because a person's foot or leg was so badly crushed between two machines that they could not be mended. (There's nothing quite like an ambulance driving into the center of the warehouse to pickup another accident victim.) Recently, we had a new employee who had just started his first day of work and who was training on a piece of equipment. He left work in an ambulance. He crushed his foot between two machines and had to have his foot amputated. (I later found out that infection had set in after the surgery and he had to have the same leg amputated to just below the knee.) *"Welcome to Lowe's Regional Distribution Center #965—where Safety is first and foremost!"*

Those were just a few of the irritants working at Lowe's. But the number one irritant for me was the demeaning attitude of management and the actions of a few "favored" employees of management as well. (We actually had a couple of laid-off aeronautical engineers working at Lowe's doing the same kind of work that I was doing, so I'm not totally alone in my perceptions.) I'll be fifty-five years old next month. I've had forty years of experience in the workforce. In that period of time I've worked in construction, repaired vehicles, installed electrical systems and plumbing, worked with customers, and learned a lot about computers. Somewhere along the way I attained a Bachelor of Science degree, served two separate tours of duty for over thirteen years in the Army, raised two wonderful children, and held positions in laborer and management. I've been a supervisor, a foreman, a leader and most recently at Lowe's … a slave. In my spare time I've tried to help others, taken on causes that I felt were important, and even wrote a book. I'm opinionated and I can be outspoken at times. But mostly, I want to take pride in my work and feel like I've accomplished something worthwhile. I won't be treated in the manner of S.O.S (another acronym for sack of shit) or allow others to be treated that way. I believe in human dignity (and frailty) and that everyone has something of value that they can contribute to the whole—that each is an integral part of the process we call "work". I believe that steers have a purpose in life and that queers are without purpose—and I know the difference between the two. And if I'm standing in the soup line at Cheyenne a month from now I hope that all of what I have accomplished was a worthwhile endeavor. And that's how I feel.

THIS AND THAT

Fall is definitely in the air here in Wyoming. Each night is much cooler now and the other morning we received a faint trace of frost on the windshields. Michel continues her work at the Lowe's Regional Distribution Center but I can honestly say that I don't miss that place one bit since I left there. In the meantime, I am now self-employed and I've started my own business working out of our home here at the ranch. I am laying the groundwork for what I hope will be a profitable business. Many things still need to be accomplished to get everything completely up and running, but everything is falling into place nicely thus far.

Telephone service continues to be one of my biggest headaches. I now have a Toll-Free number for my business in addition to my regular phone number. But I still need some additional services that I presently do not have. Hopefully, those services will be taken care of in the coming week. (I utilize my computer for a majority of my business but the connection speed is so slow that I may have to resort to a satellite provider when the business foundation is on more solid ground. There's no such thing as "cable" in these parts.) Right now, two tin cans and a tight string are the best I can hope for. The telephone company is supposed to be upgrading its services here sometime in the future. Maybe that will at least provide a faster connection speed.

On the days that Michel works I'm up at 4:30 in the morning, so my day is just as long as her day—though not as demanding physically. (I actually feel much better now that I've left Lowe's.) My time is allocated towards my business here at the ranch with phone calls and computer work so I don't get outdoors as much as I previously did. I guess that will be okay once *Old Man Winter* sets in. My Dodge truck was in the dealership for three days this past week so that they could do some warranty work on it. (I've had a continued electrical problem with the number eight coil pack on the engine resulting in an engine fault.) I've got the truck back now and so far everything is still working okay. Ah … the computer age!

Other than that, not a whole lot has changed. I'm enjoying the fall season—it's hard to believe that summer is gone. Soon it will be rifle hunting season. Maybe I'll take some time off and see if I can get close to any antelope. Who knows, I might get lucky and one of them could jump out in front of me. The presidential election will be here shortly. I've decided that I'm not voting for President Bush or Senator Kerry. I'm going to do a "write-in" and vote for myself. Of course I won't get elected … but at least I'll be voting for someone I truly believe in.

CHRISTMAS AND COWBOYS

Christmas and Cowboys. An unusual Christmas for me. Here at the ranch it's hard to imagine what Christmas day will be like. It's hard just imagining what tomorrow will bring. The wind has been incessant for several days now. What snow has lingered has been blown back and forth so many times that it is wearing itself thin. The prairie grasses are brittle and gold. The stars at night are bright and luminous—constellations and constant reminders … of our fragility. My fingers crack and bleed from the dryness and my daily work. I wear the dust from long hours of working in this outdoor life. Bed time comes late for me—too late because I stay up too long and get up too early. I sleep out of weariness and not out of peacefulness.

Christmas and Cowboys. Feeding out hay, breaking ice in the water tanks, riding my horse in the frigid morning hours and hoping I don't get tossed from the saddle while I'm stiff from the cold. Brilliant sunrises and sunsets with the mountains in the distance. And always … nature embraces me. Moonlight in my room replaced by dark nights with firelight emitted from the flames in my stove casting shadows about my castle on the prairie. Would I trade this way of life for something better? And what would be better than the life I presently live? A stuffy building filled with stuffy people? A hustle and bustle hell-bent-for-leather-going-nowhere job where I have to meet someone else's expectations? I'd rather be a poor cowboy than a wealthy nobody.

Christmas and Cowboys. I no longer know if I can be of any comfort to anyone, or that I should be. I wonder at times what really constitutes "loss". Did I ever really have anything to lose to begin with? Christmas is but one day out of the year. But each day that I live out here by myself is a lifetime. I lose track of time—days of the week and today's date. I lose track of … myself. The prairie is like the ocean's vastness and I am but a small vessel sailing these rolling plains. I need an anchor. I miss a loving companionship—someone to share life with. I've been alone for so many years now that I sometimes doubt my own rationality.

Christmas and Cowboys … a way of life—and my choice.

TURBULENT TIMES

It's been turbulent times for me lately. Two weeks ago I injured my back working in town lifting heavy spools of wire weighing over a hundred pounds each. Something in the center of my back snapped and that was that. It took two separate visits to the chiropractor's office to repair muscles and realign my spine—and two weeks to recover. Last week I added to my pain by getting in the middle of a dog fight here at the ranch which resulted in a bite to my upper left arm. I still have teeth marks and bruises but I can at least lie on my left side when I sleep at night without too much trouble. If I turn over the wrong way, I wake myself up. In the last year I've lost ten pounds—down to one-hundred-and-forty pounds now. I eat like a horse and consider myself healthy, but that type of weight-loss concerns me. I've given thought to leaving the Cattail Ranch for employment elsewhere, or to move into Cheyenne to be closer to work there. A ranch in Encampment, Wyoming is presently considering me for the position of ranch hand supervisor of their operation there. I don't know that I would accept the position if it is offered to me. The money and additional fringe benefits would be good and better than what I'm presently making, but moving either to Cheyenne or to Encampment would require me to leave here, and I don't know if that is the right decision.

Michel doesn't want to move. I've been working with a realty company in Cheyenne. They have available housing that I've looked into that will accommodate Michel and both dogs with no problems. I haven't done much around here at this ranch these last two weeks because of my back pain. We're presently cutting hay and getting ready to bale and I'm able to move around again without too much trouble, but I go back to town to work tomorrow for the next three days of twelve-hour shifts. I'd better take it easy working in town this time around.

My personal life isn't much better. Michel has made it abundantly clear that she has no plans to marry me anytime soon—if ever. She says that she cares for me as a person but that love is a totally different issue. I reckon I'm still a free spirit, and the engagement ring I gave to her on Christmas day was a bad investment on my part. (I'd been better off buying some more tack when I bought my new roping saddle—at least the horses would wear the stuff.) In this man's estimation, she'll always remain a wonderful gal though.

We did go to the theater together last night to see the movie *Fahrenheit 911*. It turned out to be worth seeing. If you're a Democrat you'll like the movie. If you're undecided about the presidential election this might help you in your decision-making processes. If you're a Republican the movie will first of all piss you off, and then make you want to leave your party and go over to the Democrats. And if you really don't care, then you'll be in good company with the majority of Americans that never vote but bitch every time they're government does something not to their satisfaction. They really have no reason to complain when they don't vote.

By Sunday of this past week, both my back and arm were still bothering me. I decided that work was going to be too painful so I headed to Denver to see my daughter instead. She had oral surgery—having her wisdom teeth cut out. She looked like a chipmunk but she was well into the recovering process. We went to a couple of restaurants to eat and watched a movie at her apartment. We spent some time together as a father and daughter should, and we had a good time. I had not been to Denver since October of last year and I was in need of another dose of "Rat Race" medicine. I got my share of medicine driving in those parts of uncivilized humanity. It makes one appreciate driving on a dirt road, dodging cattle and antelope and slinging cow manure on the side of one's truck. I don't believe the residents down there in Denver appreciate a driver with a cowboy hat, driving a Dodge truck with Wyoming license plates. It must irk them when they see someone that doesn't fit their definition of normal. I do get a great deal of satisfaction irritating those kinds of people and it made the trip worthwhile for me.

I don't know what constitutes "turbulence" for you personally. To me it's just the crazy ups-and-downs in life, the non-caring attitudes of some people, or a corporation's lack of concern for the well-being of their slaves that they call employees. Maybe it's that incessant pain that won't allow one to either work or sleep. Perhaps it is to love without being loved. The "measure" of a person's character is not what that individual has encountered in their lifetime; rather—how they have dealt with it instead. Like a good game of poker, I'm still in the game … ready to play another hand. I never know what cards I'll be dealt, but if I fold now, I'll never win a game.

Part Two—Still Kicking

Zack Wellington had found the high, arid and undulating plains of Wyoming to be compelling. He recalled the countryside of his native New Jersey, where just recently he had graduated from Princeton. Life there seemed somewhat less harsh than the ground he was now lying upon. He pushed himself into a sitting position and the world around him spun out of control. His head felt as if someone had attacked him from behind with a hammer while his backside was sore from his butt cheeks to the base of his neck. Prickly pear cactus was embedded in the palms of his hands—the buttons now constant reminders of how "personal" this Wyoming landscape had become. Blood was dripping from his nose and splattering mosaic patterns on his shirt. His hat, jeans and boots were covered in dust. Meanwhile, several hundred yards away he could see his horse still on the run—bucking away. And if that weren't enough, Jim and another man were now curiously approaching him in the distance. This morning's start wasn't a good one.

Zack's father had told his son that he had lost any vestiges of sensibility when Zack had announced after graduation his intentions to work in Wyoming during the upcoming summer season. But Zack was in need of change and time away from the curriculum that had consumed so much of his personal life recently. Perhaps a change in environment and work would help him to adjust to the rigors of obtaining his degree and pursuing law. Mary Wellington had sided with her son and his decision to seek work in the west. Money was not an obstacle in the Wellington family. Why not let their son enjoy a little diversity in his life for a change? Besides, he would return home in the fall, hopefully to further pursue the Wellington family's interests.

Jim spoke first.

"Zack, this here is William Johnston, owner of this outfit."

Bill didn't waste any time with introductions.

"I don't mind paying a man for a good day's work. Matter of fact, a little rest once in awhile is due to those who've earned it. But I don't particularly appreciate those that earn their wages sitting down on the job, which appears to me to be exactly what you're doing right at the moment. And to top it all off, you took one of my good horses out of the corrals and let the critter go wandering about the prairie like you don't have a care in the world. I think a little explanation is due from you son."

Zack staggered to his feet, trying unsuccessfully to steady himself. The world took a sharp turn and down he went. He shook his head clear and tried again, this time with a bit more success. Still wobbly, he peered at Mr. Johnston who was returning his gaze with a sharp expression. Damn it all. His first day on the job and he was about to get fired.

"Sir … I really don't have any excuses for what just happened. I … ah, kind of lost control of the horse and I apologize. I'll go out and get him back for you real quick like."

"See that you do," Bill replied. With that said, he turned and walked away towards the main house.

Jim did his best to suppress a smile. This boy had sand even if he had no sense.

"We'll go and get two other mounts and gather up your horse before Mr. Johnston changes his mind about you working here. You okay, Zack?"

"Ah … yea Jim, I think I'm a little better than I was a few minutes a go. My head still hurts like hell and this cactus doesn't feel too good either. Other than that, I feel like a new man.

Jim laughed at the appearance of the blood-splattered, dusty silhouette of a boy before him and recalled the days of his earlier youth when he too had eaten dirt. Wasn't life just once great escapade after another?

"Get your hat and let's go get that critter before he tears that saddle up he's still wearing. After we get back you head on over to the bunkhouse and clean yourself up. The cook will be ringing that dinner bell here shortly."

The two of them headed towards the corrals with Jim in the lead. Looking back, Jim watched as Zack veered first one way, then another, and finally straightened his course to match that of Jim's. Further in the distance Jim could make out Zack's horse that had by now finally settled down and was grazing peacefully along the stream's edge.

"Zack, I told Mr. Johnston that you had previous experience with horses and with cattle. I hope that you'll not let me down when it comes to moving cattle."

"I'll do my best, Jim."

"Good enough, Zack."

Reaching the main house, Bill chuckled silently to himself. For a college grad this kid was well educated … but not all of his lights were lit yet. He liked the way the young man handled himself though. Most kids his age would have blamed the horse for what had happened. Bill knew better. Dusty was a tough but good cutting horse prone to tantrums for no apparent reasons at times. He had found his rider's weakness and felt his uneasiness in the saddle and had quickly dispatched him. Better men than Zack had been tossed off him, and most had no further desire to renew that relationship. But Bill sensed that Zack was different than the other previously hired hands. He would soon find out.

INDIAN HILL ROAD

Indian Hill Road weaves with the tapestry of the landscape. Hard and dusty when dry and greasy when wet, it shares its inconsistency with few travelers. Here, hawks perch atop fence posts then sweep in front of the infrequent vehicle. The high plains in September with warm days and cool nights and the mountains in the distance, add to the solitude and grandeur of every sunrise and sunset. This home of mine shares its place among old foundations, buildings, corals and broken machinery of yesterday's past. Bits and pieces litter the site as relics of what once was. There was an old hay wagon with a television sitting on its dry and weathered bed when I moved here, uniting the past with the present. I pitched the television set for a more favorable view of the hay wagon. One will find on the ground rolls of rusty barbed wire intermixed with the mellow sounds of distant cattle and swaying grass all united by the prairie wind. Changes in the weather can be viewed from a hundred miles distance. And always, there is the unlimited sky that reaches from one horizon to another.

A few days ago I moved the cattle from here north on up the road about five miles or so to a different location. Just me on horseback pushing the cows and calves towards better grazing, and so now it's quieter here than it was before. My daily entertainment occurs during the morning and evening hours when I'm feeding seventy Hereford bulls and attempting to keep my thirty-pound buckets in hand while selecting a route on foot through the hungry boys. When I drive up to the four separate pastures and they see me coming … the race is on as to who can reach the feed bunk first. I've got my favorites in each of the pastures. They too have personalities just like people do, and don't mind me scratching their backs or playfully pulling their horns. However, their gentleness is a bit rougher than mine. If they get too rough or start a fight I throw an empty feed bucket at them and they scatter like kids on the school ground. I know later they will change personalities when they leave here to take up residence at other ranches like the Cattail Ranch where I previously lived, but it is fun to have them around even though they're still big and rambunctious boys. It's hard not to like kids.

They're just good old boys that eventually go on to other pastures. The bulls and I share similar traits and dispositions and maybe that's why I get along so well with them. Sometimes the world closes in so tightly that it's hard to breathe. One loses objectivity and individuality and in the process ... loses one's self. I may not have stored up much in this life of mine in the way of possessions but I'm not ready to lose my soul just yet. I ain't real sure what a cowboy is supposed to be ... but I sure as hell know what he isn't. I can't live where the streets are paved and the neighbors look into each other's windows. I'm not particular to laws or to governments and I never want to be a burden to anyone. I respect the rights and freedom of each individual and I feel it's a damn shame that this country has stooped so low to think it can dictate individual freedom and expression by mass media coverage and political agendas.

You do your thing and I'll do mine, so goes the song. Right now, here on Indian Hill Road, life is okay for this ol' boy. But I know there will come a day when it'll get too complicated and too congested and then it will be time to move on again. I've been alone so long that I'm not sure I could live with anyone else. In the meantime ... I'll try to get along with myself.

DOWN TIME

I had traveled back to Indiana in October of last year to visit my family. My mother did not want to see me at all, so I abided by her wishes. My brother explained that she was not feeling well and did not want "visitors", so I returned to Wyoming. When I moved back to Indiana in April it was pretty much the same thing. Mother didn't want any "visitors" though that did not apply to other members of the family.

When I left Indiana in June of this year I felt it best to leave the past behind as well. Bitter feelings are best buried so I left without leaving word with my family regarding my departure or future destination. As far as anyone was concerned, I was still living and working there in Martinsville. Family relations being what they were (and still are); nobody there had any intention of maintaining contact with me on a regular basis.

I usually "stir the pot" when I get a burr under my saddle so I sent off an email to my sister-in-law, *"Anybody looking for me? I'm not where you think I might be."*

I got an email response the following day from her, *"Yeah you dumb ass I have been trying to track you down for over 2 months now. I have tried internet, phone records, your sister in Lafayette etc. I have been trying to contact you to tell you the latest news though not good at all. On July 2nd your mother passed away and I have been trying endlessly to find you. She was in pretty bad health for 2 weeks and she went down hill quickly, it was rather sudden. Where have you ventured off to this time? Suppose you don't have a phone do you? If you do you can call or e-mail for more details. Good to hear from you finally. It really has had me stressed out that I haven't been able to find you to tell you the sad new. Write Soon!"*

I sent a short reply, *"Thanks for making me feel better with the 'dumb ass' remark. I have no desire for any further details regarding Mother's death. She will always remain my mother. <u>Thank you</u> for letting me know though."*

With that family (that I grew up with) who needs friends, right? But I remember the good and so easily have forgotten the bad. In my book, *Considerations—Emails From the Heart*, there is a dedication page that reads, *For Mother … Who taught me the Joy of reading, and the "Art" of expression.* I had signed and mailed my mother a copy of my book when it was first published, but I don't know that she ever read it. I reckon it doesn't matter anymore. The last time I saw her was before that book was published.

This week, three months after my mother's death … I finally receive word of her departure, and still wish the wounds to heal. I told my boss here at the ranch that I needed some "down time" when asked if I would work this Sunday. So far he hasn't called for me. Some wounds go too deep to heal properly, so you have scars as evidence of improper healing. And while my body still has the physical scars from past events, it is the mental scars that continue to hurt more deeply.

I don't have all of the answers and probably never will, and if my family from childhood days still doesn't know of my whereabouts then that's okay too. Some things are best forgotten … even if it's me. But that dedication I wrote for my mother was written from my heart, and I hope that now she knows it. Finally, I wish her the joy of her own *down time* … with dad.

COWBOYS AND DOGS

Cowboys and dogs make pretty good partners and they share a lot of similarities. We enjoy chasing cattle, though we'll deny that was ever our intent. (After all, it's just our natural instinct that if something is running you just have to go after it.) We don't mind wearing a little cow manure once in awhile but unlike dogs, cowboys try not to make a habit of rolling in it. We both have received our share of kicks from hooves but still laugh at the close calls. *"Missed me, you sorry___!"*

When cowboys and dogs get excited they both howl and when in the company of one another, they sometimes howl together. That's a combination I've always found entertaining. Of course, neither one can carry a tune, but that doesn't matter because it's fun anyway. Neither the cowboy nor the dog is suited to city life. If a dog howls in town then somebody is going to call the fuzz. And if the cowboy howls in town then he's going to see the fuzz. Nope, the best place for cowboys and dogs to howl is right out there on the *ole prairie*.

Both cowboys and dogs have eaten their fair share of dirt. The difference is that for cowboys it was mostly unintentional. Both like to go exploring and when we find something that we like, we bring it home with us. It matters not that what we found has little value. We found it, it's ours, and we're taking it home. And when we're done with it, we bury it so we'll never find it again. Both of us know that it's around here ... somewhere.

Cowboys and dogs sometimes prefer things that are not good for them. They can enjoy bad places more than good places because bad places get attention. (After all, we eventually get thrown out of the bad places anyway.) Doing something bad is the easiest way to get recognized. That's why you don't see too many cowboys or dogs in church on a Sunday morning ... it doesn't get us the attention we're looking for. We do a better job of communicating with the *One* up above when we don't have ceilings or walls that block our view of the mountains or the plains. I reckon cowboys and dogs have a preference for more natural settings.

Cowboys and dogs share a fascination in discovering old bones. Both can visualize the creature that previously gave form and substance to life that has now gone on to better pastures. The cowboy and dog will tilt their heads with quizzed expressions searching for answers, then look at one other. Both share the same conclusion resulting in a *"beats me"* expression. But they wonder just the same.

Wondering and wandering seem to be a way of life for the cowboy and the dog. Maybe because they share a way of life and many similarities is the reason they get along so well. They can speak to one another without ever saying a word.

STEAK PLEASE

The first contact that Max had with a human being was when searching hands reached into his mother's uterus. Max was being pushed out of the security of his mother's warm body and had somehow got himself twisted-up in the process. Now this pair of hands was gently aligning his front legs beneath his head and pulling him where he didn't want to go. Damn—that was one hell of a departure from his mother's body to this cold hard ground! This sure wasn't "life" as Max had known it. Mom's tongue was all over him now. Outside it was snowing hard and the wind was blowing something fierce. But here inside this barn it wasn't so bad. At least the new mother and calf were inside from the weather.

Wobbly legs and mom's uttered insistence finally got Max to the milk faucets. Hey—this wasn't bad! Days later with warmer weather Max and mother were cajoled into the outdoors and joined the rest of the mothers and their newborns. All of them were pushed into a different pasture. March rolled into late April and mothers and calves were moved into a small corral and separated. A cowboy walked into the small corral shortly afterwards. (Some of the calves made sure to give the cowboy a good beating for this uninvited entrance. A couple of good kicks to the legs and one good kick to the groin for good measure!) Max felt his left hind leg leave the ground as he was being hauled backwards out of the corral towards the branding fire. Up and over, he hit the ground—one cowboy at his head and holding his front leg close to his body with a knee on his neck, while another cowboy held onto his tail and shoved Max's left hind leg forward with one boot while the cowboy's other boot was planted squarely over Max's rear end. Horns pasted and hot iron applied to his hide—Max was up and out of there ... but he got even with that cowboy on the tail-end when his boot slipped off. Max made sure that cowboy would wear a little "rear-end" perfume for the remainder of the day.

A month later Max didn't feel so good. Max had the scours. A couple of cowboys pushed and prodded him from his mother and got Max into a chute. Then one of the cowboys jumped in there with Max, put his thumb in Max's lower jaw, yanked his head back by the nose and shoved a couple of large pills down his throat. A week later Max was back to good health once more. Late spring all of the mothers and their calves were moved into another range. Life was good and Max enjoyed the entertainment activities of the other calves. He followed a couple of them through some broken wire in the fence line one day but then he couldn't figure out how to get back to his mama when it was dinner time. This was not good. Fortunately, a couple of cowboys came along on horses and opened a gate. Then they prodded Max and the other calves through the gate and back to their mamas. Rap, rap, rap ... staples driven into newly stretched barbed wire and the hole was closed.

It was October now. All of the cattle were gathered up and herded into a big corral. Max and the other bull calves were separated from their mothers and hauled-off in trucks miles away from the life they had grown accustomed to. Cake, hay and the year's remaining grass was now their diet. The scours got a hold of Max again with the new diet he was on. Back to the chute. A cowboy climbed in with Max and tried the same routine with the pills. This time Max had the weight advantage and gave the cowboy a lesson or two by slamming him into the wall a couple of times for good measure. But the cowboy still got the pills down Max's throat. Max was his old self again in another week … but the cowboy still hurt. The cowboys got even with Max and the other bull calves a couple of weeks later when they were "banded" and transgressed over into "steer" life. Hay wagons and sixty mph winds, frigid temperatures and horizontal snow storms. Six-inch ice in the mornings on the frozen water tanks. Cake, hay and brittle winter grass. Muddy corrals when the sun melt the snow during the day and the hard cold ground at night to sleep upon.

Winter progressed into spring and the warmer weather returned once more. Salt blocks, cool refreshing water in the water tanks, fresh grass and wide-open skies beneath the stars at nights. This was the life! Mid-summer with flies on the hide. Drying land and sand in the eyes. Oily scratchers and slowly turning windmills—hot winds during the day and cool breezes at night. Fences mended and the rounds made. Vehicles repaired. Hay cut, raked and baled—and loaded into the stack yards. July turned into August and then it was October again. Fall roundup and Max and the other steers loaded into trucks and off to feeder lots back east. Heifers weaned from their mothers. And the process begun all over again. Dust in the eyes, ears and mouth. Manure on a cowboy's clothes as prideful testimony of hard work and a five-hundred dollars a month paycheck. Sore muscles, stiff joints and cut hands. Chaffed backsides from saddle time. Dust covered Stetsons, worn leather gloves and grimy bandannas.

Cowboy: "I'll have the eight-ounce steak cooked medium rare."
Waitress: "Sure … What type of potato would you like?"
Cowboy: "Fries would be fine."
Waitress: "What would you like to drink, Sir?"
Cowboy: "I'll start with a whisky … straight-up."
Waitress: "Hungry AND thirsty—that's my kind of cowboy!"
Cowboy: "Believe me ma'am … I've earned it!"

SADDLE TRAMP

I'm nothing but an educated saddle tramp. I graduated from high school but I'm still befuddled how I ever got a degree from the university. I reckon I'm higher up on the saddle tramp hierarchy because I can't fit everything I own in the back of my pickup truck even if I did decided to hit the road. (I'd still have to rent a U-Haul trailer to haul all of my stuff. Now that is *class*!) I like cattle, horses and dogs, however I have no luck whatsoever with women. Even *eHarmony.com* says I'm a lost cause.

But I am fortunate in having a full-time job. Unlike some folks who work five days a week with weekends off (I call them *part-time* employees) I work seven days a week with no days off, which makes me a full-time employee. And I have a lot more employee benefits than most folks do. I don't punch a time clock every-day for one thing. My boss knows where I am day or night whereas most bosses don't care where you are when you leave work at the end of the day. I deal with *stock* from sunup until sundown, without the use of brokers or the internet, and I directly influence their outcome. I can dress anyway I want when I go to work. The only dress code I have is to try and be comfortable. I don't belong to some union or pay dues just so I can have a job that sucks anyway.

My work requires safety at all times. No need to worry about some idiot doing me harm. (I just have to worry about this idiot.) Besides, if someone were dumb enough to injure me in my line of work I'd have every right to get even with that individual. In this line of work we really do look after one other, because what goes around comes around. I can swear, smoke a cigarette, or spit anytime I feel a hankering to do so. (The cattle don't seem to mind.) Oh sure, I get muddy, dusty, rained and snowed on at times. I even get cold in the winters and sweat some in the summer. But I'm outside where it doesn't matter, not in some office, nose to armpit with other employees. I don't have to try and get in some exercise to stay in shape because I get to work-out everyday ... for free.

I have no paperwork to push around trying to look busy or justifying my exist-ence to the boss. I have no desk with a name plate on it identifying who I am. The way I figure it, others either know me, or it's their loss. I don't make a lot of money on my salary, but then I don't need a lot of money to *live*. I don't have to schedule a vacation because my vacation time is whenever I'm *not* working. I get to see each sunrise and every sunset, listen to the birds, breathe fresh air, watch the wildlife and view the wide-open sky daily. No office job can offer that! And I can set my own pace because I have two speeds. (If you don't like my present speed you sure as hell won't like the other one!)

I don't have to worry about being charged with sexual harassment, racism, or preferential treatment because I'm the only hired hand at this ranch. I can call the old cow a bitch and get away with it. (She doesn't know what I'm saying anyway.) And if she doesn't do what I want I can kick her in the posterior, ever mindful that she can kick me back if she wants to. Now, that's fair and equal treatment.

I have a revolver, a rifle and plenty of ammo, a bottle of whisky in the closet, cold beer in the refrigerator, Dish TV, my own surround sound, a radio, DVD/VCR player, and broadband … all on the job site. Oh yea, my home is on the job site as well so I don't have to commute back and forth to work. I can call the boss anytime day or night and he can do the same if he wants to get a hold of me, which he does from time to time. And I get daily job recognition. I don't have to wait for some review to find out how I'm doing.

At the end of a day's work on horseback I have what no office employee will ever have. I get a horse that nuzzles me with affection thus forming a real *partnership*. But I didn't have to go to some university to learn about all of this stuff. And I didn't get it in some book or a video. No sir, I got my education with on-the-job training instead. I never did get a certificate or a diploma. I reckon being a saddle tramp is an on-going education.

ANOTHER WEEKEND

The newspaper stated that around 3,000 acres were burned this past Saturday. I don't know how you measure acreage burnt when fire engulfs hillsides covered in scrub as well as prairie. The newspaper also reported that the multiple fires were started intentionally. That part of the story I agree with. Word on the ground was that kids were igniting books of matches and throwing them out of their vehicle along the frontage road by the interstate. The smoke was deceiving in terms of distance and location when viewed from afar. Up close it was more personal.

Overhead, the chopper continued its aerial observation relaying to the units on the ground the direction of the fire. When I arrived, the fire had begun to crest the hilltops in front of us, shooting thirty-foot flames and towers of smoke into the air. This was not a broom and wet gunny sack affair and the units on the ground knew it. One chance to end it all lay at the bottom of the hills at the edge of the prairie. Fire trucks and crews spread out along the line. The command was brief and to the point. If the fire could not be checked, our route of escape was to go north and away from the blaze.

In the west, the sun was an orange ball of hell veiled behind a solid curtain of smoke, and the dark and ominous flames continued their advance towards our line of defense. The smoke intensified and the wind began to shift direction. Just before the wall of fire reached the bottom of the hills the wind died to a gentle breeze. The crews went into action with water trucks up and down the line dousing the fire's leading edge. Now it was dark and one could see other fires still burning within the contained area. Nine o'clock on a Saturday night and for me, it was time to go home. Winter pastures saved. I read about it in Sunday's paper and thought the story was rather lame compared to actually being there. It's difficult to be personal … from a distance.

Sunday morning I reached a decision. I had been pondering for some time about sharing my life with another and I decided it was time for a change. I returned home Sunday afternoon with a new partner whose name is Louie. He's a mix of German shorthaired pointer and Border collie, salt and pepper color, and just over a year old. Louie has been in the slammer since July and was the only dog not barking when I walked up and down the rows of inmates. Actually, the folks at the Cheyenne Animal Shelter were very cordial and helpful. So now I have a new partner in crime.

Today he accompanied me in everything I did around the ranch and tonight he is worn out. Stretched out on the floor and dreaming doggie dreams, I reckon. We're getting along just fine though Louie won't let me out of his sight. He's a gentle and affectionate companion and presently this man's best friend. Friendly towards others but protective of me when I'm with the bulls, so I have to keep an eye on him so he doesn't stampede the livestock. We're both adjusting to one another but we should encounter few problems. After all, it's a dog's world … and it takes one to know one.

A Sweet Song

The days are shorter now, and the nights longer. Sometimes I sleep well at nights, and then there are those hours of darkness when slumber occurs only in my subconscious mind, and I wonder if I've slept at all. It must have something to do with the season. My dog Louie provides me constant companionship whether I seek it or not. I can't always take him with me during the daytime hours so he sleeps on the floor beside my bed each night so that I'm never out of his sight.

I've come to the conclusion that Louie is a terrorist, so I have added to his name. I now call him Louie Bin Laden. My front yard looks like it belongs to Sanford and Son. Everything that is trash ends up in my yard, thanks to Louie's scavenger efforts. Like Bin Laden, he can be in the immediate vicinity and I can't see him because like a terrorist he blends in so completely with his surroundings. He has destroyed nearly every toy he has been given, from Frisbees and balls, to an assortment of chew toys that he has shred to pieces. He has dug holes in the yard that I have refilled only to fall into again after he has re-excavated them. I believe the dog is out to finish me off. I hate him and he hates me and that's why we get along so well. Companionship.

I tire easily of the same routine. So does Louie. Each night I have to conjure something up for my evening meal, which I sometimes share with Louie so he won't eat me in my sleep. I only have two television channels, one out of Cheyenne and one out of Casper, and both are worthless. But that's okay because I only watch television for the news and weather. Here in Wyoming there is no news and you can usually count on the wind blowing so it only takes a few seconds to get up-to-date with both. I find it ridiculous that it takes anywhere from thirty minutes to an hour for the television folks to figure these things out. When it's all over I wonder what the hell they just said, and why I even watched it to begin with. It must be a routine.

The prairie grasses are now brittle and the cold seeks out my weaknesses. I find more comfort watching the sun set behind the distant mountains as the kaleidoscope of colors transcend to somber hues of darkness. If it's not too cold, I'll take a short walk during this transition and listen to the evening breeze. Of course, I have to deal constantly with that four-legged terrorist trying to break my reverie (and my neck) by tripping me up with his playful antics. I never know when I might end up face down on the ground because Louie Bin Laden has successfully executed another sneak attack upon me. His feet will bounce off my back as he dashes off in another direction seeking another avenue of approach to get my attention.

He now knows how to howl and growl. (I taught him how to do both.) He'll even watch television if he's bored. Louie likes Chris LeDoux music in the background when he's reading the newspaper or one of my books. If he doesn't like what he's reading then he eats it. I like that idea of eating something that irritates you. I even let Louie Bin Laden edit what I write. (If you don't get this latest dissertation from me it's because Louie ate it.) One thing I haven't let Louie do is to share my beer. I don't want empty beer cans littering my front yard.

I don't need a lot of that city stuff. No traffic or disruptive noises in the middle of the night. No sirens or noisy neighbors. No human sounds whatsoever. What I do need is a little understanding. Since I already know that a little "understanding" is hard to come by, Louie Bin Laden accomplishes that for me when he does his growl-howl, as only he can do. Somehow it doesn't quite sound like "dog" but instead … a sweet song.

PARTY LINE

Mother's Day has come and gone. My mother was still alive during Mother's Day last year. The two of us rarely agreed on anything, but I dedicated my book to her anyway. Growing up as a kid back there on the farm in southern Indiana I learned a lot from my adopted parents. Dad was a combat veteran of World War II and fought across the Pacific as a Navy Seabee. His last island was Okinawa before we dropped the "Big One" on the Japanese. He was glad of that because he wanted to come home to mother. Mom was sixteen when she married dad and before he left for the war. They didn't see each other for several years because of that war. Dad was proud to have fought that war because he was an American. Mom was just glad to have her husband safely back home. My grandpa Jordan served in the Army *and* the Navy. I thought I could fit in somewhere between the Army and the Navy so I took my military physical for the Marine Corps back in 1968 before I graduated from high school. Several years later when I did eventually join the Army I called my Dad and told him what I had done. There was a long pause on the other end of the line, and then he said … *This is a Navy family*!

A pause on the line was a regular occurrence back there on the farm. We had a *party line* that we shared with two other families just up the road from us. Back in those days when someone called you the phone rang at the three separate family households. The caller would tell the answering party who they wished to speak to if the wrong household picked up the phone. Common courtesy dictated that if the call was not for you that you dropped off the line. You kept your calls shortened so as not to tie up the phone for the other two families, in case they needed to use the phone. If you wanted to make a phone call you'd pick up the phone and sometimes hear one of the other families talking on the phone so you would quickly and quietly hang up the phone so as not to disturb them. Unless … you were Betty Burns, one of our *party line* families. Betty wanted to know what was going on all of the time. You'd hear that familiar "click" on the line and most likely it was Betty listening in on your conversation. My mother would get so mad that she would tell Betty to get the hell off the phone! "Click". (Mother had a way with words.)

Everyone on our *party line* knew phone courtesy because of that saying, "*what goes around comes around*". We knew that other folks' conversations were private and didn't concern us unless you were Betty Burns or … today's National Security Agency (NSA). Betty Burns wasn't the sharpest knife in the drawer but she was smart enough to figure out that the other two families on the *party line* weren't terrorists. Today, many Americans are willing to sacrifice their privacy and to surrender individual freedom with one another, all in the name of fighting terrorism. I for one am not! That's not what my grandpa or my father fought for in taking up arms against the enemy. That's not why I served my country either.

Are we to line up like cattle going to the slaughterhouse? Whatever the current administration tells us we are to believe? I love this country and especially its people so much so that when that final day rolls around for me and I leave this earthly existence it will be because of a broken heart. All our individual freedoms and hope for the future forever vanquished. Once taken … it will never be returned. "Click".

PEACE AND SERENITY

I miss some things. Peace and serenity for one. When I had my phone line installed with Qwest I thought I missed the internet, but I was wrong. (The internet was the main reason I had the phone hooked-up.) I don't have to have the internet or a phone ringing every time some computer-generated machine dials my phone number wanting to know if I'm home while I wait for a salesman to come on the line trying to sell me something I never asked for to begin with. I don't need the viruses, Spam, pop-ups and the myriad of other bull shit the internet provides on a constant basis.

Effective this Friday November the 4th I will no longer have a land-line phone or dial-up internet service. No more annoying phone calls. No more email address. No more out of pocket expenses for either. I won't need to look at the answering machine every time I arrive home for missed calls and disconnects. I've only had the phone and internet service for a little over a month and already I've had enough. Peace and serenity will be their replacement.

Some folks won't know of my discontinued service because they never read my emails. (I've always believed that proper etiquette required some kind of a response, even if was just a grunt.) This world is moving too fast. When I was a

Captain in the Army one of the favorite sayings from the higher-ups was to, *"Slow down the train"*. My response was, *"Slow it down hell … the damn train is derailed!"* The higher-ups didn't like that, and I didn't care. Don't pretend to be the damn Engineer when you don't where your caboose is.

I've been dragging ass for a long time now. That doesn't mean I'm not working hard. It just means that I'm tired of a lot of things. The local news is now focusing on the flu pandemic that is going to hit the world population. There's no vaccine currently available to fight this virus. Even if they can develop a vaccine it will take at least six months to do so and the health authorities estimate that by then over a million Americans will be dead. You may not hear from me but I won't be dead. No sir, I'll stick to my cold remedy of two aspirins and a shot of whisky every half hour. It may not cure the flu but I won't give a damn! Anyway, I'm tired of these so-called "authorities" and their medical and other opinions.

This country is filling up, even here in the least-populated state of Wyoming. It's getting so that you have to look around before you can "water the grass". (If you're not living and working out on the prairie this won't make any sense to you.) It seems that wherever I travel, civilization follows. Even when I was in the mountains up above the timberline I'd find some lost hiker stumbling onto me wanting to know what time it was. I say "lost" hiker because if they're asking for the time of day then they should have never climbed the mountains to begin with. The whole idea of climbing the mountains was to get away from "time".

Maybe it's time to move on. Too much of anything can be too much. Too many phone calls, too much internet, too little caring about others. I don't want to lose the important things in my life by concentrating on those things that drag me down. I'd rather head for the high country and towards peace and serenity. Take care, Partner. We'll meet again on the flip-side. Cowboy Up!

Part Three—Coming In

Coyote Sam was crouched in the limestone rocks watching the scene play out in the valley below. A rider had just eaten dirt and his mount was heading towards Sam's location. Sam knew the horse would eventually stop long before he would reach his position in these rocks, but he still worried that he might be seen. In the minutes that followed, Sam watched as two men approached the rider sprawled on the ground. One of the men turned and walked back towards the ranch buildings and the other two men were now heading towards the corrals. Sam had earned the title of "Coyote" many years ago when there were bounties still available on the creatures. He was good at his trade in those days—now long gone. The coyotes were still in abundance but there were few bounties available and the funds usually ran out before any real harvest of hides could be accomplished. Sam never went for that poisoning process—he deemed the whole thing as a rebuke to his talents as a marksman. He preferred clean and humane shots from a distance. As the years had rolled by, even the poisoning process had been eliminated by the government. The forties and fifties seemed like eons ago. Now it was the sixties and the times—*they are a changing* as the song goes. Coyote Sam had to make adjustments as well. Taking odd jobs here and there just to make ends meet. He still preferred the wide-open areas in this vast part of the west and he still roamed where his heart took him. But he was getting old now and he needed some funds to get him through the upcoming winter months. Living out under the open skies in the dead of winter was a young man's sport and much too hard on this tired old body. Drifting had become a way of life for him but recently he sensed, more than felt that his drifting days were fast coming to a close. So he had taken to rediscovering the haunts he had known as a younger man, coming back to a region he knew so well many years ago. This valley had not changed much in those intervening years—a few more buildings and people, but not much more than that. He still rode when he could have driven one of those new-fangled automobiles instead. A horse could go where no automobile could and Sam didn't want to tie himself to civilization. Besides, he didn't want to submit himself to a state's licensing procedure in order to drive something with wheels. He supposed that someday some government bureaucrat would come up with the bright idea of raising more revenues by requiring horsemen to obtain a license before saddling up their mounts—a "pleasure" tax they would call it.

Sam straightened and stood up. Stiff from squatting so long—knees and back popping as he moved off in the direction of his horse grazing just on the other side of these rocks. He knew a family that lived in this valley but had not seen them in the last twenty years or so. Sam's reputation was renown in those years. Most of the ranching families welcomed his presence back then when he was hunting coyotes. Many of those same families were more than willing to take him on as a hired hand during those days when he wasn't hunting, as Sam was a hard worker and could "cowboy" with the best of them.

"Yo—Biscuit, come here boy … time to get going."

The horse raised its head and nickered back at Sam. Biscuit was an older bay but still a good horse. He nuzzled Sam's stomach, working his forehead up and down Sam's chest as Sam tried to reach for his reigns.

"Knock it off you old galoot. Time to go meet some folks. You can acquaint yourself with the other ponies when we get down there. Damn it Biscuit—you're going to knock my ass on the ground if you don't stop that! I ain't no scratching post!"

Sam rubbed behind Biscuit's ears and deftly followed down his neck until he had the reigns. He patted biscuit's neck then swung up into the saddle. Seems like his whole life has been in the saddle. He swung his horse's head around and headed out of the rocks and into the valley below.

Liz was at the kitchen sink finishing peeling the potatoes for the dinner meal when Bill entered through the side door. She glanced at her husband and smiled. Bill's arms encircled her waist from behind and he gave his wife a gentle hug.

"How's the new boy working out?" she asked.

"That feller from the east has a few things to learn about horses. Jim and him are on the way out to gather-up Dusty. That horse just laid him out on the ground."

"He's not hurt is he?" Liz asked.

"Naw—but his pride sure took a pounding. I reckon he'll be alright. I had a few words for him afterwards."

"Now Bill, don't you go and start getting tough on that boy! He comes from a good family and first impressions will mean a lot to him."

"Yes Ma'am."

"You don't have to be so calloused with the hired hands either."

"Yes Ma'am."

"And stop that 'Yes Ma'am' stuff ... before I crack you up the side of the head with this potato peeler!"

"Yes Ma'am—err ... I mean yes dear."

"Who's that?" she asked.

"Who's what?"

"That rider coming down from the hills in the south?"

Bill peered out the kitchen window in the direction Liz was looking. A lone rider was slowly making his way down the steep hills in the direction of the ranch buildings.

"Well, whoever it is I don't recognize him from this distance," Bill answered.

Spook and Lucky, the two ranch dogs, immediately started barking and were already running to investigate this new arrival.

"Guess I'd better go find out who it is," Bill drawled out.

"Guess you'd better mosey on out there mister," Liz replied in a comical tone of voice. She gave her husband a kiss on his cheek.

"Dinner will be ready in about an hour—don't be late! Be sure to let everyone else know too."

"Yes Ma'am."

Liz chased her husband out the door ... potato peeler in hand.

INTERNET RETURN

Returning to the world of the internet could not have been accomplished without the assistance of Buck Holmes and his wife Eva Jeanne here at the *R Bar H Ranch*. I now have internet access via Broadband, and a much improved means of communication. And I am grateful, to say the least.

Spring brings hope in Wyoming. A warmer climate returns, the daylight hours begin to lengthen and the grasses sprout green with the arrival of newborn calves. I enjoy this part of the earth's cycle. However, things just wouldn't be right if we didn't jump our clocks ahead during the process.

Everyone needs a jump-start once in awhile. When the battery goes dead an extra shot of juice can do wonders. Perhaps that's what I need, an extra shot of "juice". Cruising the internet and getting back in touch with friends by email can do wonders for one's soul. Writing letters is more personal and is in many ways a lost art for a lot of folks. But then, thirty-nine cents doesn't buy much these days either. Actually, *nothing* really buys anything nowadays.

Maybe we should go to a bartering system and trade-off those items we no longer need for the things we would like to have instead. (There are a lot of things I'd like to have but when checking my inventory I come up short on the bartering end.) A favor for a favor is about the best I can do. *That* doesn't cost anything, means a lot more, and is remembered forever.

ANGLE IRON BUNKHOUSE

Angle Iron provides strength. Welded, it supplements flat steel. Tough stuff by itself, it's even tougher when reinforced with additional layers of iron. "Angle" is sometimes defined as a *point of view*, while "Iron" is known for *great hardness and strength*. Maybe my opinions are derived from hardness and strength. Then again, I could just be another *Wacko*. (It matters little if I am affiliated with one or the other.)

I've often thought that the ideal bunkhouse on a ranch should be made of steel, supplemented with *angle iron* for extra strength. The construction of such a bunkhouse would prevent many ranch hand residents from burning, bending, or breaking what they have been provided for in the way of housing. The ranch hand would likely suffer personal injury in attempting to dismantle his home while in a self-induced drunken stupor. (Of course, the following morning he would have to explain to the boss how he acquired the multiple bruises from the previous evening's activities. To which the boss might reply: *"Rough night? I noticed that the Bunkhouse didn't suffer though!"*)

Combining my opinions and sometimes my "bunkhouse mentality" gave credence to the idea of a new email address: *The Angle Iron Bunkhouse*. A bunkhouse known for being tough, indestructible, full of opinions and … my kind of place. So if I bruise myself in the writing process, it just goes with the territory. It might not be pretty but it could be effective. It may hurt like hell when it's all said and done but I get to toss my ideas around. And I get to toss myself around in the process while sharing my thoughts with some special folks via the internet.

BLOOD UPON THE DUST

The moment I squeezed the trigger my life changed forever. Like watching events unfold in slow motion, the deafening blast, the recoil and it was over except for the memories. The nightmares, cold sweats, screaming out in the deep darkness, all give credence to my own personal insanity. There is no honor in death. There is no honor in killing. There is no honor ... but in living.

Brown hills and ragged blue mountains in the distance, canyons and glacial lakes, a whispering stream of ice water in this desert world. In the distance the steady thumps of rotor blades ... choppers looking for targets. They do not endure my sweat, the dust or the loneliness of this landscape. Nor will they comprehend the earthliness and peacefulness that two feet planted upon jagged rock give to one's soul. They only see it from above.... but fail to touch my own reality.

Blood upon the dust, cracked wind and burned face, an olive drab bandanna around the neck, cool breeze upon charcoaled skin freshens one's hope and spirit. How I got here is more important than where I am going because I don't know if I'll ever return to any home again. Sanctuary is in the mind. I'm so tired that I don't care if I live or die. I just want rest now. Somewhere to lay down and to dream a thousand dreams ... away from suffering. Hot and pulsating flesh, a bullet wound radiating heat from torn tissue. Is it shock or hemorrhage? It doesn't matter. What matters is that I'm still alive. I clinch the rock-dust in my fingers and lean back against the cliff's face, in the cool shadows where the choppers can't see me.

This is *freedom*. Some find it and give their lives for it. Others have a vague notion and are in constant search of it. And others dream of it. But I ... I live it. A world away from everyday experiences that are so drab, so predictable, so rational so like living ... a slow death. I am *gone*, if ever I was there to begin with. I was a boy once, with boyhood dreams and hopes, and faith in my elders. But no more. My faith is within myself. Only I can live my own life. I ask for no one's blessing or understanding. I no longer care.

I caress my rifle and my *Savior*. After my days in the Army there was this life that I now reflect upon on. Unstructured, unobtrusive ... unforgiving. Wounded soul seeking peace and understanding and eventually fitting into the *norm* of things. So young, so distant, so damn *wanting* to find the world around me! Rock shards from exploding ordinance derived from overhead. The choppers ... those damn choppers! Seeking my life, my very existence in this world. There is no dress-right-dress in these mountains. No pressed uniforms or military formalities such as saluting or polished boots. No marching bands or starched behavior. No military flourishes or political speeches about *duty, honor and country*.

God forgive me ... for I have lied to myself and to others. I am a Judas in disguise. There is a home for me somewhere. A place where I can dream a thousand dreams in a land far, far away. A place to sleep and to rest. Where there is no war, or daily battles. No hostile action. No loss of sensitivity. My chin slowly descends to my chest and my breathing becomes shallow as my eyes close. Far away the choppers leave my conscientious as I sink into the base of the rock supporting my back. I dream a thousand dreams of wide-open skies, a cool breeze beneath the shade of cottonwood trees and my blood is no longer upon the dust.

ENEMIES

Well over a month ago a thunderstorm rolled overhead with little warning here at the ranch and then lightening struck the broadband antenna at Buck's home and cooked a couple of routers inside his house, his computer, and some other electrical equipment as well. Unfortunately, I wasn't ready and by the time I got to my Dell laptop computer to unplug everything it was too late. The electrical charge had traveled the hundred yards or so down my Ethernet cable to my laptop and took out the laptop's microprocessor as well. Good bye laptop! No computer, no internet, no email. Been kind of quiet around here since then. Until yesterday … when I went into Cheyenne and purchased a new desktop system. My life story it seems, but once more, I'm up and running. (*It's hard to keep a good man down.*) I've got my digital camera, a computer system that works, and my thought processes that have never been sharper, depending on one's perspective. It just doesn't get any better than this!

Unless … you tune into the news and what's happening around this world of ours. Same old … same old. People killing people. Just can't get along with anybody anymore. I have been described in many ways by different folks. I've been called *rowdy, obstinate, belligerent* and most recently, as the *devil* himself. But I haven't killed anyone … lately. (I did shoot and kill a badger for Mrs. Ruppert over on Indian Hill Road the other day.) Mostly, I've just put up with all of the pests in my lifetime … and there have been plenty of them! I do have a problem with puckering-up and kissing someone's rear end just to make them happy. If I call you "Sir" or "Ma'am" it's out of respect and not because of some slobbering fearfulness of you.

It seems to me that everyone is looking for a new enemy. We just can't be happy with old enemies … we have to find some new ones. If we spent a quarter of our time looking for new friends instead of enemies we'd be a lot happier. Most people we label as our enemies aren't really our enemies. We'd just like them to be enemies so we can justify hating them, for whatever our personal reasons. Is that screwed-up or what? I really can't think of anyone that I really hate. Pests ... yes but hate, no. I know how to deal with pests.

When I visited my son Thomas a few weeks ago, and before I headed on down to Denver, the two of us went to old town Fort Collins. We browsed the shops in the old town section and I finally found a shop that had bumper stickers. I found a bumper sticker that kind of said it all for me; *We're making enemies faster than we can kill them.* So I slapped it on the back bumper of my truck. When I returned to the ranch I showed that bumper sticker to Buck. He looked at it for a couple of seconds then said something about it being a "liberal" statement. I replied that I didn't know if it was a liberal or a conservative statement ... that it just seemed true to me. Buck reluctantly admitted that yes ... it was true. And I didn't even make an enemy in the process!

GOOD MUSIC

I like good music. Unfortunately, there's not much of that available on today's radio or most of the present store-bought CD's. I've been accused of enjoying country music and I do ... some of the time, but not today's country pop-trash. For instance, I totally dislike the music of Tim McGraw and despise his synthetic black plastic cowboy hat. (He can't sing either.) I enjoy some light rock and a few of the older rock classics. I even at times enjoy the sounds of symphony music, but I don't like getting too depressed. Bluegrass is okay until it gets too tangy. If the music doesn't pick me up then it's basically a let down.

The only music that keeps me hopping is Celtic. I especially enjoy Irish music—both vocal and instrumental. I listen to http://www.live365.com whenever I have the opportunity. My internet radio presets are *Celtic Quest, Celtic Highway, Celtic Journey, Celtic Melt, and Highlander.* Of course, one needs cable or broadband capabilities for adequate buffering and listening enjoyment. I then plug my computer into my surround-sound system and tune into the Irish station of my choice. Wham! I'm right in the Irish countryside or one of the local pubs tying to keep the beer in my mug. (That's hard to do when one is dancing around in the middle of the living room.) It seems I'm always kicking those bloody leprechauns out of my way!

My philosophy about music has always been that if the sound doesn't make you feel good then it's not worth listening to and you might as well turn it off. (Sometimes *silence is golden* if there are no other choices at hand.) I know that everyone has musical favorites and whatever turns your crank is fine by me. What turns my crank is what touches my heart … and good Celtic music does that for me. I imagine a whispering stream, blue skies with fluffy clouds, a cool breeze, the sun setting behind mountain peaks, and a good woman to dance with. Some would venture to call that heaven but I enjoy thinking of it in terms of reality.

Presently I'm tuned in to *Celtic Melt* as I'm typing this. When I get tired of typing then I'll get up and dance a jig, grab a beer and then get back to typing again. It's one of the few times that I don't mind doing two things at once—listening to music and writing at the same time. No one is gnawing on my ear or trying to get my undivided attention while I'm plugged into this land far, far away. Why is it that when you're enjoying a blissful moment there are those who would like nothing more than to dash your processes and to interject themselves into your presence. Get out of here you damn leprechaun! Can't you see that I'm enjoying my solitude? No … get your own beer and leave mine alone!

If it works on your mind then you rationalize it—but if it touches your hearts then you have to believe in it. Music lifts the soul and my soul has needed a lot of lifting at times. No … I'm not depressed. And I won't get depressed as long as I don't have to listen to someone else's interpretation of good music. If I have to bang my head against the wall just to get the beat I'm going to be in bad shape because I don't have a whole lot upstairs to begin with. In the meantime I'll stick with some good Celtic music and may the *Luck o' the Irish* be with you!

HIPPIE COWBOYS

I had a few losses this past year. I lost my mother, my dog Louie who I put down on my own accord, my Dodge truck, and my girlfriend Michel. (I miss Michel the most.) But I'm not down on my luck just yet. I did my Federal Income taxes the other day utilizing Turbo Tax. Fortunately, I had already received my W-2's from the Cattail, Berry Herefords and the R Bar H ranches, and Kelly and Adecco temporary services. I was still trying to get my sixth W-2 from Rogers Group, Inc. whose corporate offices are in Nashville, Tennessee. They wouldn't send me a W-2 without me filling out their request for a W-2 and enclosing a copy of my driver's license with the request. I had saved my last pay voucher and I did a little research and got their EIN (employer identification number) and went ahead and filed my taxes. I'll be getting a refund. Then I sent some tornadoes back to the Nashville area as a little retribution for the bull-shit they gave me. I give back accordingly to those who deserve it. *Don't screw with me!*

I still remember lifting each of those heavy cement blocks on that Rogers Group production line back there in Martinsville, Indiana. Hour after hour, enduring humidity, the heat, slave-labor and a less than worthless tit-less union that didn't allow for any rest breaks or lunches but was quick to grab your union dues every payday. One day, as I was moving each hundred-pound block into position on that production line, I looked through the open bay doors and viewed a beautiful blue sky and white clouds above and I thought to myself; *"What the hell am I doing here? That looks like Wyoming sky to me. I'm out of here. You don't even have to kiss my ass goodbye!"*

Buck and I went to the Wasatch Gun Show yesterday in Cheyenne. I bought some more ammunition for my .45 Long Colt Single Action Army revolver. I feel comfortable with that sidearm. That caliber has been around a lot longer than anyone living these days and it still has enough knock-down power to put you on your ass and keep you there. They don't call it the *Peacemaker* for nothing. The dealer wanted to sell me some .45 LC Hollow points. I replied; *"What for … these solid lead, flat-tipped round nose bullets have been around for over a hundred years and have worked well all of that time."* (Just once I'd like to have the opportunity to shoot at someone who had some intelligence!)

Yea … losses seem to tally up for me. But I'm grateful for so many things that have come my way. Like the great folks I've worked with on the ranches I've lived. I've always enjoyed sharing experiences, bickering and even getting drunk with the other ranch hands. Working hard and playing hard. *You may own my body but you'll never own my soul!* (You may not agree entirely with me … and that's okay too. I'd wonder about anyone who thought the same as I do.) I'm a *Free Spirit* and I don't plan to change anytime soon. Cowboys in the past were *Free Spirits* too! Back in the 60's we'd call those with a free-spirit … *Hippies.* Times, they are a changing, and today they are a dying breed.

I must be getting older, as I can think of no greater honor than to be known as a *Hippie Cowboy.* The only respect I have for others is for those I know. And if I don't know you … it's your loss. *Saddle-up and ride hard partner!*

ILLEGAL IMMIGRATION

I'm tired of the illegal alien problem. In every instance that we attempt to rationalize or work through the problem of immigration, from the president to congress, from rancher to fellow neighbor or from friend to foe, we continue to miss the real meaning of American citizenship and the one correct solution to the problem.

This country still remains the greatest nation on earth; why else would anyone wish to come to this country if it were not so? But we tend to forget our own lessons in history. (Some of us have a problem just remembering what happened yesterday.)

Nearly a hundred years ago the immigration problem was addressed in a most eloquent manner and our present-day politicians would be much better off in their decision-making processes if they would just open their history books and read a tad bit more. The following quote basically sums up the illegal alien problem for me, and I hope it will for you as well. I fail to see why present times are so different from the past.

"In the first place, we should insist that if the immigrant who comes here in good faith becomes an American and assimilates himself to us, he shall be treated on an exact equality with everyone else, for it is an outrage to discriminate against any such man because of creed, or birthplace, or origin. But this is predicated upon the person's becoming in every facet an American, and nothing but an American. There can be no divided allegiance here.

Any man who says he is an American, but something else also, isn't an American at all. We have room for but one flag, the American flag. We have room for but one language here, and that is the English language and we have room for but one sole loyalty and that is a loyalty to the American people." Theodore Roosevelt (1907)

JUST A RANCH HAND

He's just a ranch hand. Adopted and raised in the Midwest, he first came to the Wyoming territory thirty-eight years ago. Then he left for parts unknown. Somewhere along the way he worked his way through college and graduated from the university with a Bachelor of Science degree. He served in the ranks from Private to Regular Army Captain—an appointment made by the President of the United States. Three Honorable Discharges later with some medals, and assignments from Asia to Europe and parts in between, it was time to concentrate on family. The end result produced two wonderful children and a divorce.

It took him forty years to locate and meet his sisters and brothers by birth when today most families barely spend forty minutes together. His closest sibling by birth is a sister a thousand miles away who doesn't make pretensions and who understands her brother out west. He's just a ranch hand—who loves the land and those that graze upon it. Loyal even to those who have stabbed him for pure vindictiveness, in understanding what they will never comprehend—that loyalty comes from the heart and not the mind.

Money doesn't make the person, but hard work does. Sometimes one has to pay the price along the way. Scoliosis of the spine, flat feet, disjointed collar bone, and arthritis—to name a few. No matter the ailment, he still shows up for a full day of work on time each morning. He could be a saddle tramp or a drunken bum at first appearance. Dirty jeans, torn shirts, worn leather gloves, scuffed boots and an old hat are often his work attire. Nobody has seen him dressed-up for years now. But then for him, there's no occasion to dress-up for. He's just a ranch hand.

He's nuts about good music (a little on the loud side), good food and companionship that could possibly last his lifetime. He never figured that he'd ever get to the age he is now. Along the way he has given of himself—to the extent that there have been financial losses, lost friends, and physical pain. Today's blessings include a good horse to sit upon, fair weather and a comfortable bed to sleep in at night. There's always tomorrow. Every day is different and unplanned for him. Whatever the boss wants. As a ranch hand, understanding cattle is easier than understanding people. He knows what cattle want and need.

He's had plenty of other jobs. Some were good-paying ones with good benefits. He knows that as a ranch hand you're paid a monthly salary and expected to work with no benefits except maybe housing and some food. He's doesn't know how his pay goes from monthly to hourly when he needs to take a day off once in awhile for a little vacation. But then he does know that as a ranch hand it isn't about the job. It's about a way of life.

He knows the value of a good fence and that every fence has two sides to it. One side keeps the critters in … while the other side keeps the critters out. He's never figured out why most folks can't see their own lives as fencing—keeping some in and keeping some out. After all, most fences are supposed to be shared with others. He knows when that old cow gets on the wrong side of the fence that he has to go after her. The old west had no fences and few boundaries. Today there are a lot of pitiful fences with too many boundaries. You either think like you're expected to think or you're an outcast. He's proud of his accomplishments, proud of his work, and proud of the folks he's known. But then … he's just a ranch hand.

LOVE ... DAD

At times I find difficulty putting my thoughts into words. My thoughts arrive hard in this oftentimes cruel world of ours. So much bitterness profusely spread by so many individuals intent on demeaning the character of others. Hard to believe that there can be so much hatred spread by so few. My most precious moments are those times when I have the opportunity to reflect on the happiness of others and what they have brought into this contemptible world. I know there are many people better off than me, and yet I am amazed at how despicable they are towards others and how self-righteous they are in their all-assuming attitude.

There is neither a king nor queen's ass on earth worthy of me playing homage to! (That goes the same for the president, congressman or a multimillionaire.) There is only *One* that has my complete loyalty—and he alone will pass judgment upon me when my final day comes. You can judge me for whom I am but I am still me, like it or not. *I am what I am and that's all that I am.* I would rather die a violent death with a bullet through my heart than to live life in humility and servitude as a slave to another. I would slash my knife across the jugular of my enemy than to reward him with menial and condescending compromise.

By now you're probably wondering to yourself if I've finally flipped-out and finally gone off the deep end or something. (You need not worry; I went off the deep end a long time ago.) I have tasted the bitter fruits of life and come to enjoy their flavor, so many years ago. I admit it—I'm addicted. My daughter recently sent me some pictures of her cats that she loves and adores. By chance she also enclosed a picture of herself with her cats. There are Picasso's and Rembrandt's as works of art—but there is only one *Amanda*. And fortunately, I am her only father.

I was born Melvin Hood. I was adopted at six months of age and raised on a farm in southern Indiana amongst the Jordan clan. It took me over forty years to find and finally meet all of my other six brothers and sisters. I eventually traced my family heritage all the way back to England. (My family arrived in Virginia and eventually migrated to Kentucky, where I was born.) Upon his death, my birth father could neither read nor write—he would never realize that one of his sons would become a college graduate. I am proud of each and every one of my sisters and brothers! I am proud that this nation gave my family this *opportunity*. I am proud of my heritage, and I am proud of my son and daughter.

There are those so subtle moments beyond history and heritage that are most important to me. The rare moments that breathe life and meaning into one's soul. The saying goes that *a picture says a thousand words*. And so it is in the early morning photo of my daughter, surrounded by her loving cats. *Wake-up ... wake-up Punkin, the critters are calling! It's time to forget yesterday's bitterness and animosity. Forget the outside world for the moment and instead focus on the most important things about you.* The greatest riches in your life surround you. *Give ... and you shall receive.* And above all—love those who love you in return. Love ... Dad

WEDEMEYER FIRE

Over a week ago there was a grass fire just south of Whitaker Road on the west side of the interstate. Buck and I arrived on scene first and we knocked it out before any other units were required. It only burned about a quarter of an acre. But I still remember helping with the Cattail Ranch fire back on the 6th of March in which (according to GPS estimates) 1,064 acres burned. We were fortunate in both fires, though I know its little consolation for the acres of forage lost.

Today was a different story when a fire call came in this morning requesting assistance to Platte County and the Chugwater fire departments. I don't know if you or Rod know Russ Wedemeyer just north of here up towards Chugwater, but their house caught fire. Laramie County Fire District #2 responded along with the other units from Chugwater. Buck and I arrived on scene with Brush-25 (B-25) and assisted in fighting the house fire. (The high winds we had today were horrible!) Everyone fought the fire both from inside and outside the Wedemeyer's home until late this afternoon.

It was a sad day for all. Mrs. Wedemeyer was in tears. Once the fire reached the attic of their two-story home and got into the roof it was touch-and-go then. Their home had probably been added on to and remodeled throughout the years which only added more dense material for the fire. At one point I thought we had a chance. We had plenty of firefighters, equipment, water and foam, but it was not to be the case. Once the fire got into the roof it spread and became very intense and then several hours later we had to get all of the firefighters out of the home and off the roof because the roof was ready to collapse. We salvaged what we could for the Wedemeyer family by carrying out family heirlooms from the burning home before the roof caved onto the second floor.

The main reason I'm telling you this Mae is that the Wedemeyer's had left their home for only about an hour this morning. It appears that they had some baby chicks on their back porch and were using some kind of heat lamp or incubator to keep the chicks warm. That's where the fire started. It went straight up the wall and into the attic. I'm not trying to lecture you and I don't know if you're raising any new chicks this year over in the west chicken house, but if you are and have the heat lamp(s) going you might want to make sure someone checks everything for any possible fire danger.

After Laramie County Fire District #2 departed, Buck and I stayed on scene in case any grass fires got started from the house fire. We left after the Wedemeyer home collapsed inward to the foundation and the Chugwater fire units felt there was no longer any grass fire danger.

Give my regards to Rod and the rest of the gang there at the ranch. I know everyone is busy there with calving as we are here.

LUCKIEST MAN ALIVE

I've gotta' to be the luckiest man alive! My fifty-seventh birthday is Sunday and I'm happier than a pig in shit. Buck gave me the day off today and a bonus pay-check to boot. I went to town and lived it up. I replaced the ignition module in my Chevy truck, bought a new black Stetson hat for gussing-up purposes and a new twelve-gauge shotgun for four-legged varmints such as skunks and badgers or two-legged varieties that I don't want to deal with anymore. (I put that shotgun in the old 1968 Ford truck's gun rack that I drive around the ranch.)

I've gotta' to be the luckiest man alive to have been blessed with a beautiful daughter and a handsome son (both who still love their old crusty bastard of a father) and with an ex-spouse who put up with my crap for twenty-three years and gave me such wonderful children, while enduring Army separations and hardships. I talked to both of my children tonight. Thomas leaves for Hawaii on the 1st of November for a three-week backpacking excursion by himself and will be back by Thanksgiving. (I think I bred an *Explorer* in my son.) Amanda has my fiery temper and crazy sense of humor—and my blue eyes. Other than that, she's her own person.

I gotta' be the luckiest man alive to have survived my little shooting excursion today. I took that new single-shot shotgun of mine out for a test drive this afternoon. I took a handful of #1 steel shot shells and loaded up some three-inch high-velocity magnum rounds that leave the barrel at 1,450 feet-per-second. Damn near knocked my shoulder off its hinges after two rounds! I obliterated my targets at thirty yards, to say the least. I just hope that in the future I continue to hit what I'm aiming at with the first round because I have that feeling there's going to be more pain on my end than on my target's end. I've got a nice bruise and a throbbing shoulder for all of my efforts—this through four layers of clothing. God I love the pain and the thrill of it all!

I gotta' be the luckiest man alive to have a home with a roof over my head, food in the frig, a good bed to die in every night, a good boss, a good cuttin' horse, plenty of ammunition, and an occasional whisky to ease the pain at day's end. Julie, (the gal that helped me pick out my new Stetson hat today) is absolutely gorgeous. A beautiful woman with a charming personality—and married of course. (You can bet there's a lucky man in her life!) I felt like I was eighteen again today. I may die in the morning but at least I'll die happy.

I gotta' be the luckiest man alive to have lived as long as I have and to still be in relative good shape. I'm just a little guy with a big heart—my dad always told me that *dynamite comes in small packages.* I believed him. When I go I want to go with a big bang and take as many of my enemies with me as I can. The *old man* also told me that *the bigger they are—the harder they fall!* I'm still seeing living proof of that today. I've stumbled a few times in my life but never fallen. I love this life of mine—it's ALL mine! I gotta' be the luckiest man alive!

FIRE IN THE EYE

I've often believed that there's a fine line between courage and stupidity. Facing a towering fire can humble the bravest and give credence to the fool. These last few nights for me have been with little sleep and late hours breathing soot and ash. A few days ago the Nimmo fire raced across the prairie heading west—three blackened fingers reaching for the interstate while the north and southern flanks attempted to sprawl outward. Then on Thursday night we were assisting Platte County with a fire (west of Chugwater and south of Wheatland) that had raged for several days due to another lightening strike. Nothing like the Nimmo fire, this fire was into the mountainous hills, trees and heavy brush country. You didn't go after the fire—you waited for it to come for you.

Near the old Dilts Ranch, I stumbled up into a steep canyon full of cottonwood trees and piles of dead brush as the blazing inferno roared towards me blowing its hot breath and ash before it. My only weapon was a high-pressure hose in my gloved hands and our own *Brush 25* truck behind me as this devil towered thirty feet above me spouting flame and cracking overhead. Further behind us was one ranch house nestled beautifully in the cottonwood trees and directly in the path of this roaring bastard of a beast. I looked the Devil in the eye and spit on him!

I was with Buck Holmes (Captain 25 of Station 5) and our only partners were *Brush 24* with Ed Weppner (Captain 24 of Station 4) and Tracy Almquist as later the darkness of night settled in and we watched the crawling fire lines creep up and down the mountainous terrain before us. The Chugwater units had already pulled out for rest. (They had been fighting this fire since six-o'clock the previous night and were in much need of rest.) Every time the fire reached another Juniper it took off like a Roman candle shedding light across both sides of the valley we were in. The wind shifted from the west and started coming from the east. And we waited while evaluating our possible route of escape.

All volunteer firefighters without pay or benefits. Unlike the despicable and worthless bastards that are careless with cigarettes or fireworks in this drought-stricken part of Wyoming, we care about out neighbors—their homes and family members, livestock and grazing lands, and we take appropriate risks to ensure their safety. Our reward is the *thanks* we receive from those in saving their home or their way of life. I detest the emergency pager call in the middle of the night. I deplore the ride out to the unknown. I hate those who wreck death and destruction on innocent others through their careless and stupid actions. But once I am upon the ground with my fellow firefighters my only fear is not being able to overcome the beast before us. I guess all of that is why I volunteer—to do what I do.

Later, as we sat in our brush trucks watching the flames etch across the blackened landscape before us I told Buck that I wish I had brought some dogs and some beer. It would have been a fine weenie-roast. He just laughed. Never take yourself too seriously or think that you're unbeatable. Nature has a way of reducing even the most pompous ass to that of a menial moron. Laughter and volunteering are both good medicine if you give a damn about others. Otherwise, get the hell out of the way while we look the devil in the eye.

ON YOUR OWN

A few nights ago I was awaken around midnight from a deep sleep with another pager call filled with static. I got out of bed and turned on my two-way radio to receive additional details regarding the page. The radio was filled with static as well. I couldn't understand a damn thing about the call! My cell phone did not ring so I figured that the call wasn't for us or otherwise Buck would have called me. (I found out the following morning that Buck hadn't heard the pager call.) I finally got back to sleep about a half-hour later. I've had folks ask me why I even do this firefighter stuff. The next morning after another restless and sleepless night I made my decision—I told Buck I was resigning from Laramie County Fire District #2 and that I was no longer going to be a firefighter. He took it well, asking me if I was tired of the bullshit. I wrote out my resignation that very day and packed-up my firefighting equipment.

As volunteer firefighters Buck and I are on call twenty-four hours a day, seven days a week—unlike those volunteers who live in Cheyenne with regular jobs and who decide what hours (after their regular job) they would like to be on call as a firefighter. I found that after a long work day and dead tired I was called out along with Buck for either a real emergency or just another bogus call that someone decided to call in. Sometimes we wouldn't return home until late at night or the early hours of the morning. But no more—at least not for me. Buck went on another call yesterday without me to the same residence we had previously gone to a couple of weeks ago for an unreported controlled burn. Same scenario, same address, but a different moron this time. This time the damn idiot damn near burnt down his whole neighborhood!

I've lived most of my life without asking for the help or assistance of others in most instances. That old saying of *you saddled that bronc … now you ride it* holds true for me even today. Evidently, most of present-day society can't wipe their own ass without the help of someone else—to which I now reply; *you're on your own now!* And so it is with fighting fires—you're on your own. Don't call or come crying when it's all gone. If my place burns down then I'll just start over—just like I've done all of my life. After all, my home is the outdoors the majority of the time. As for volunteer firefighting … you get what you paid for.

This morning's haze was contributed in part from the *Big Timber* fire up in Montana blowing this way. (It will only get worse here as we move into this fall season.) I'm not being vindictive in my decision—just realistic. I still pay tribute to the volunteer firefighter in my written resignation.

September 5, 2006

Subject: Letter of Resignation

I hereby tender my resignation, effective this date, from the Laramie County Fire District #2 for personal reasons. During the time I have been with Station #5 I have enjoyed both the duties and responsibilities of becoming a firefighter, and especially working with Captain Buck Holmes and the other firefighters of this district. Throughout this period of time I have come to realize the unique personal qualities of each firefighter in this district—their dedication and tenacity in saving lives and property ... and I salute each of them!

Few residents of Laramie County totally comprehend the volunteer firefighter's fortitude in dealing with emergency calls both day and night ... every day of the year. Fewer residents give due recognition to those same volunteers who place their own life in harm's way in saving the lives and properties of others. In the best or worst of times the firefighter is always there.

I wish to thank each and every firefighter in this district for the opportunity of serving with them. And while I may no longer work with such an honored presence of firefighters you may rest assured—you are not forgotten!

Respectfully,

Ron Jordan

THE BRIDGE

Some things I'll never understand. I am reminded of the story of the old cowboy who had lived a long and hard life riding throughout the western United States and who remained faithful to his wonderful wife for many years. That old cowboy's appointed day finally arrived and when he reached the heavenly gates the Good Lord smiled at him and said, *"You have lived a good life—do you have any final requests of me?"* The cowboy thought for a minute or so then replied, *"You know Lord, I've been riding that horse of mine all over the west but I've always had a hankering to see Hawaii. I was wondering Lord, could you build me a bridge from California to Hawaii so that I might take one last ride on that cowpony of mine?"* The Good Lord thought for a moment then replied, *"You know son, considering the amount of materials involved, the number of workers, and the amount of time to build that bridge, I think it would be better for you to request something else."* The old cowboy gave some thought to the Lord's advice. Finally, the cowboy said, *"You know Lord, I've been faithfully married to the same woman for many years now but I've never really fully understood her. She has the strangest mood swings. For example, she cries when she's happy and laughs when she's sad. Lord, could you please explain to me what goes on in a woman's mind?"* The Good Lord thought for a minute then replied, *"You want that bridge to be a two-lane or a four-lane highway?"*

I try to understand many things, even with my limited intelligence. Midterm elections are just days away and the media is going full blast giving their own analysis of the projected outcome—Republicans versus Democrats, conservatives against liberals, and the good guys taking on the bad guys. (Like any of that will make a difference once our elected officials reach Washington.) I reckon that things won't change that much for me, though millions of Americans will stay up late on election night viewing the results and seeing if their *wishes* come true. As a registered Independent voter my choices are limited to the lesser of two evils when it comes to voting. The horses and cattle don't give a damn about the elections—they just wonder if I'll be on time with their oats and hay in the morning. I've never had a candidate ask me what I thought or what they can do for me once they reach Washington. I always thought that was what politics was all about—taking care of your constituents' wishes.

I guess I'm just *out of touch* and *out of mind* in thinking that any politician could possibly see things my way. I know what each day has in store for me, even if I don't know the day's schedule—hard work and long hours. I'll place my faith in a good cowpony, hope for warmer temperatures, stars to light the sky at night and a gentler breeze upon my neck. At night when I finally rest my head, I give thanks to the *One* above for seeing me through another day without too much pain or turmoil. And if I'm lucky, I'll sleep through the entire night and awaken before dawn—rested. Simple pleasures for a simple man.

Understanding is a difficult task for me. I've been digging post holes and putting up barbed wire since I was ten years old. I've worked around cattle off and on for the same amount of time. Like the seasons, politicians come and go. I've been riding horses now for over forty-seven years. Been tossed a few times and taught a few hard lessons along the way. But I still place my boot in the stirrup and hoist myself up without anyone's assistance. I reckon that bridge to Hawaii isn't really necessary. This time of the year … I just enjoy the thought of being there.

OUT OF TOUCH

Out of touch. That's when an individual judges a particular area based upon prior experience or expertise that is out of date. For example, when "White Collar" or business owners envision what "Blue Collar" employee wages and benefits should be, those doing the envisioning are usually way off the mark. (Or something as simple as when someone who is never involved with the cooking of daily meals conjures current prices at the grocery store.) Those individuals not presently employed in today's rapidly changing workforce cannot make an accurate assessment regarding anything involving industry in general. Likewise, those in industry have no concept of ranching and agricultural operations. Of course, in each of these categories those doing the conceptualization of other areas (other than those that they are presently working in) do have an "opinion" regarding those areas that are not their expertise. They are out of touch.

The days of presenting oneself before a prospective employer without resume or references are long gone. Anyone desiring to enter today's workforce should be prepared to present not only a resume and references, but to successfully pass the corporation's written tests, background checks and drug/alcohol screening, not to mention a series of interviews that may or may not result in being hired. An individual's "track record" consisting of prior employment history, actual work experience and how well that individual worked with other employees may also be verified. Each applicant competes with other applicants and only the best one gets the job.

Like the consumer who gets what he pays for ... the employer gets what he pays for as well. The employer that pays little in the way of wages and benefits gets a cheap, non-caring worker. (The better qualified worker seeks out the employer willing to pay for results and quality.) The turnover rate in today's workforce is phenomenal. But the mentality of today's corporations and private business owners is to hire a replacement worker rather to "invest" and keep the experienced worker. (I have difficulty trying to figure out why employers are continually "tearing down the house" and constantly rebuilding when they should be investing and expanding upon the existing foundation of a good and solid workforce.) When employers don't ante up to get quality with adequate compensation they ship the work overseas instead. You get what you pay for.

Every business succeeds or suffers failure due to the direct or indirect actions of its employees. That old adage of *scratch my back and I'll scratch your back* is just as true today as in years past. Employers willing to invest in their workforce will gain the confidence and loyalty of their employees. The employee will go to lengths to make *their* company the best among the competition—resulting in quality workmanship and pride of *ownership*. When corporations and business owners take care of their workforce the workforce will take care of the business. If one slights the other the snowball effect occurs and once that snowball starts rolling downhill then it's only a matter of time before the whole operation comes to a screeching halt. When either the employer or the employee believes that they know more than the other, then one or the other becomes ... out of touch. The end result is *Made in China.*

PRICELESS

Western saddle ... eight-hundred dollars. Cowboy hat ... one-hundred and twenty-five dollars. Calling the boss a stupid son-of-a-bitch ... priceless. For everything else, there's Master Card. Sometimes, I find advertising to be rather dull. Sometimes I take it a step further ... too bad we can't have truth in advertising.

I bought a 1990 Chevrolet 4X4 pickup truck yesterday. The truck came out of Nebraska. (I wonder what they do to their trucks over there in Nebraska.) It was a ranch truck as evidenced by the rusted body, cracked windshield, dents in the side panels, worn tires and the tumbleweeds packed between the spare tire and the bed's undercarriage. But it runs and it got me back to the ranch okay. I've already replaced the serpentine belt and windshield wipers. It needs a new left headlight, tires and exhaust. The 350 cubic-inch engine and automatic transmission seem to be sound. I worked on the wiring harness this morning so I would have tail lights. Anyway, it's mine and it's paid for.

If I'm lucky, I won't have to invest my next six month's pay in the old *hoss.* And if I'm not lucky, well ... it wouldn't be the first time. It's comfortable and it suits me okay. I don't have to worry about where I park in any parking lot in town. (Other folks with new cars might worry where I park though.) It's not a *fashion* statement. The way I figure it, it's not so much what it looks like but rather what it is capable of doing. If it's like me ... then it's capable of doing anything. I like the way the engine growls. I enjoy growling back at it.

I'm getting tired of hearing about all of the news hoopla regarding rising gas prices. Face it; if you have to put fuel in your vehicle then you're going to get screwed by the big oil companies. In corporate America the one who holds the purse strings dictates how you're going to live your life. *Ain't that right, boss?* It's the American way and a sad truth. That's our present-day economy. There's so much finger-pointing going on as to who is to blame that little thought is given towards any real solution.

Well, I've got a couple of solutions to our economic gas woes. First, stop construction of all those new half-million dollar homes out on the prairie twenty miles from town. That way you won't have to commute back and forth to work. (Anyone who can afford a half-million dollar home has no right to bitch about gas prices!) Secondly, if you don't like the gas mileage you're getting with your present vehicle then consider a Honda or a Toyota. If you buy American just to support our automotive industry (Made in the USA ... Not!) then you really have no excuse to complain about all of those rich camel jockeys.

It all boils down to this: New American-made SUV.... thirty-five thousand dollars. Automotive accessories to accentuate the new vehicle ... four-thousand dollars. Operating fuel cost for the new vehicle ... priceless. For everything else ... there's Master Card, because you've got no money left to spend.

ROLLING ON BY

There's a familiar chill in the air. I find myself bundling up against a cooler wind nowadays. They say summer's over with Labor Day. School is back in session with the smell of new books, polished floors, sharpened pencils and hopefully sharper minds. I've always enjoyed fall, which marks its arrival here in Wyoming earlier than it does in a lot of other places. I was born in the fall—guess I'm particular to that time of year. I reckon when my earthly existence is up it will be in the fall as well. I can't really think of a better time to go.

I finished my physical exam this last month with the Veteran's Center in Cheyenne. The medical folks there said I was in good health with the exception of a little arthritis. They did the normal blood work, x-rays, blood pressure, eye exams, prostate, cholesterol, and so forth. I asked—what about the arthritis? They told me ... *welcome to older age.* (My last physical exam was sixteen years ago when I was in the Army.) I've eaten so much rusty barbed wire that my immune system probably didn't require a tetanus shot, but they gave me one anyway. When they were done I realized that I wasn't dead yet. I figure I've got at least another twenty to thirty years left in me before I really start feeling out of sorts. (I'll have to check my paperwork though—I believe it's a *lifetime warranty.*)

Soon it will be time to gather in the cattle—ship the steers to market and wean the calves from their mamas. I've always thought it ironic that the cowhand who works from sunup to sundown each day with cattle he knows can least afford to buy a good steak for himself. I'm not complaining though. I'm just thankful I can put food on my table, a roof over my head and a warm bed to sleep in at night. At least I'm not a chicken wrangler! (If you've ever tried to herd chickens then you know what I mean. They're worse than a bunch of yearling heifers.)

They say there's another election coming in a few months. I reckon I'll vote as I usually do—for the lesser of two evils. I believe Will Rogers once said that he never met a man he didn't like. As for politicians, I've never met one I did like. I don't like *authority* either. Oh I know ... everyone has a *boss* out there somewhere, and I've had some good ones. Then again, I've had some bad ones who thought they were bosses. When they start asserting their authority that's when I show them my rear end and tell them to *boss* this!

Fall is the time of year for me when I start thinking about life's cycles. Although fall isn't here yet—it's not too far off either. We've still got some *Indian Summers* to enjoy even after the first frosts arrive. A warm vest in the evening with a good cup of cappuccino in hand and stocking feet propped up on that old coffee table. Golden leaves rustling on the cottonwood trees and burnished grasses. Horse hair a wee bit thicker and your nose running a wee bit more. (I wonder if the two are connected.) I start to wean myself from the occasional cold beer to a shot of whisky in my evening cappuccino instead.

It's a good life, though few may understand or approve. It's a reflective time for me—for what goes around comes around, and I've seen a lot come around. I plan to see a lot more. The good times and the bad ones—all created with nobody else to blame but myself. I miss a lot as the years roll on. Like a leaf floating along the water's edge, skirting the river bank and a home, I just keep *rolling on by.*

WHITAKER RANCH BRANDING

Transitioning in the West sometimes goes unnoticed by those who live in this region. Modernization and mechanization seem to rule the day. And so it is with branding. There are different branding methods and each ranch is unique in how they accomplish the task. Some load the chutes; others use a branding table, while some still use the throw-down technique. But in older times out on the prairie the tried and true method required mounted cowboys riding into the herd and roping the calves by the hind legs (heeling) and dragging the calf to the wrestlers who then threw the calf on the appropriate side and held them down for branding, dehorning, castration and nowadays, vaccinations. I have been fortunate (or unfortunate, depending on one's perspective) to have participated in all the above branding techniques.

If the amount of calves to be branded number in the hundreds and there is plenty of help on hand, by far the most efficient and effective method is roping and heeling. That's how we accomplished branding on the Whitaker Ranch on the 10th and 13th of this month. There were plenty of cowboys and cowgirls on hand for this event. There was no discrimination of men and women and their assigned duties. (We had women ropers and wrestlers doing the same tasks that the men did, and they were damn good!) When I wasn't wrestling calves I had ample opportunity to observe the work of others, receive friendly suggestions regarding my own improvement in technique, and capture the stories the cowboys told me. (One roper told me that one of their best days in heeling and branding at another ranch was accomplished when they branded eight-hundred calves in two and half hours.)

Back in my prime at five-foot nine I weighed in at a whopping one-hundred-fifty pounds. (Nowadays I'm lucky if I can reach a hundred-thirty-five pounds.) During our two separate days of branding at the Whitaker Ranch a two-hundred-fifty pound calf on the other end of the rope I was reaching for had me from the get-go, unless I used technique, leverage, and a whole lot of psychology. (Psychology didn't mean anything to the calf but it helped me to justify the idea that "I can do this!") At the end of the day I tallied up my rope burns, skinned knuckles, and dried blood marks indicative of unknown wounds, plus the various other bumps and bruises. One's adrenalin is very effective in masking personal pain during the branding process. But when it's all over and my adrenalin finally subsided, I thought a good dose of morphine would have been the best remedy for me (that and an early retirement). Cowboys never express their pain while working, even if they're losing a pint of blood an hour. Instead, the conversation might go like this: *That calf was a stocky little bastard wasn't he!* (Drip, drip, drip.)

I didn't "dress up" for the brandings. Just a white *Cattail Ranch* cap, blue t-shirt, blue jeans and work boots. I knew that I would be spending most of my time on the ground with the calves and considered myself lucky if I could get off the ground afterwards. (That's not something I dress up for.) But the real cowboys dressed the part from head to toe with hats, vests, chinks, bandannas and knee-high boots with spurs. Good saddles and good roping horses and pride in their work. They looked the part and backed it up with their actions. And I was damn proud of each of them!

I enjoyed the early morning when we all went out on our horses to gather in the herd for branding and then at the end of branding when we rode our horses down to the main ranch for the dinner meal. Man, did I put the away the grub! A lot of great food and great folks to share company with. The following are some of the folks who participated in this year's branding at the DR Whitaker Ranch:

Dave Trodstle	DR Whitaker Ranch—Foreman, Dehorning
Lesli Trodstle	DR Whitaker Ranch—Branding, Roping

Van Trodstle	DR Whitaker Ranch—Wrestler
Tracy Almquist	DR Whitaker Ranch—Branding
Julie Almquist	DR Whitaker Ranch—Dehorning
Everett Fulk (Tater)	True ADA Ranch—Wrestler
James Jordan	Iron Mountain Ranch—Wrestler, Roping
Dan Wilson	Lummis Livestock—Dehorning, Castration, Roping
Steve Beumee	True ADA Ranch—Castration
John McNiff	DR Whitaker Ranch—Branding, Wrestler
Amy McNiff	Medical Billing—Wrestler, Vaccinations
Bill Hinz	City Fire Fighter—Wrestler
Ed Weppner	DR Whitaker Ranch—Boss
Lawrence Burke	Horse Creek Cattle Co—Roping, Wrestling
Crystal Wilson	Student—Wrestler, Vaccinations
Jim Wilson	HR Fence builder—Wrestler
Dave Nimmo	Nimmo Ranch—Branding
Bob Nimmo	Nimmo Ranch—Branding
Beau Haft	True ADA Ranch—Roping, Wrestler
Richard Foster	True ADA Ranch—Roping, Wrestler
Tom Wilson	Wilson—Castration, Roping
Matt Nimmo	Nimmo Ranch—Wrestler
Jim Weppner	DR Whittaker Ranch—Branding Irons
Doug Merrick	State Brand Inspector—Roping, Wrestler
Buck Holmes	R Bar H Ranch—Branding
Ron Jordan	R Bar H Ranch—Wrestler

Thanks to those who shared their time and stories with me! Hopefully we'll all meet again for next year's branding.

PACKING MEMORIES

Growing up on a farm in southern Indiana was literally that—growing up. Most of us grow up sometime in our life. Some folks grow up earlier than others ... some never do. Who I am and what I've become has a lot to do with who I was and what I experienced in my earlier years there in that rolling countryside of the rural Midwest. I'd like to share some of those memories with you from my boyhood days.

Eugene MacInish was our closest neighbor. He and his wife were Quakers. They maintained a tidy farm and well-maintained fields and buildings. During the summer months I would help Mr. MacInish put up his hay. I remember those hot summer days in the hay fields as I lifted each bale of hay and threw it up on the hay wagon. The driver of the tractor pulling the hay wagon was always a younger kid who was too small to lift the heavy bales. Some of those alfalfa bales weighed up to 120 pounds and I invariably wore out the front left leg of my blue jeans as I used that leg to help "kick" each bale onto the hay wagon. When we had a full wagon we would then take each bale and stack them inside one of the barns. It was hot, dusty and humid work. Mr. MacInish paid me ten dollars a day and Mrs. MacInish fixed a huge dinner meal at noontime. For a ten-year old boy that was a double treat—good pay and good food. Mr. MacInish did not smoke, drink or swear. He was a hard worker, a caring husband and a good farmer. When he was diagnosed with advanced bone cancer it was already too late. Mr. MacInish endured several types of pain-killer medicines until the medicine was no longer effective. The final medicine for Mr. MacInish was morphine injections. Mrs. MacInish could not cope with giving her husband these injections, especially when the cancer progressed to where more and more injections were required. She asked my dad if he would do this for her—and my dad agreed. I still remember standing by that bedside in their farm house, watching as my father would ease Mr. MacInish's pain with another injection of morphine and watching the tears roll down Mrs. MacInish's cheeks. Finally, even the morphine was no longer effective. Mr. MacInish was a good man ... and he deserved a better death.

Ron Hamilton was one of my best school friends. From an early age, Ron had a bad heart. He had already had heart surgery at an early age. We went through high school together and sat in some of the same classes. He dated my oldest sister and I dated his oldest sister. Ron had a wonderful sense of humor. We had an economics class together and the teacher was Mr. Roberts. Ron and I would sit at the back of the class and we would prop our wooden desks against the back wall with just the two back legs of the desk on the floor. One day, Ron's desk slipped against the wall and he crashed onto the wooden floor. Mr. Rogers was irate at both of us. Mr. Rogers had a deformity in the neck region—actually; I don't think he had a neck at all. His head appeared to sit on his shoulders. Ron Hamilton would joke and whisper to me in the class room, "That Mr. Rogers is a hard-ass ... he won't stick his neck out for nobody!" Ron and I graduated from high school and the same university. He loved the game of baseball, but because of his heart condition he could never play the sport. When I was overseas in the army I got a letter from my family back home. The letter stated that Ron had been a spectator in the bleachers and had died from a heart attack ... watching a baseball game. I hope that now he's finally getting the opportunity to play ball.

The Dunnigan family settled into our region. They were a poor family. But Mr. Dunnigan was a smart man and started a business in septic tank systems. More families moved into the area and Mr. Dunnigan's business got bigger. My mother would often say, "I can remember when the Dunnigan family was so poor that they didn't have a pot to piss in or a window to throw it out of—but look at them now!" Hershel Dunnigan was the oldest boy. He was an excellent athlete and played on a lot of the high school teams. He was very popular with the other high school students and he had a bright future ahead of him. He was also very patriotic. Right after graduation he joined the United States Army and became a Green Beret, and then went to Viet Nam. The Dunnigan family was very proud of their son. Hershel died in Viet Nam ... and a lot of the Dunnigan's dreams died with him.

Max Ennis and I were good friends. Max had a way with the girls—a real charmer. The Ennis's lived down the road and were well-to-do farmers. Max had been farming since he was probably in diapers. He eventually married Denise Fletcher—the girl I had a crush for while in high school. Max went to Viet Nam too, but he came back alive. I lost track of Max as the years rolled by. One day in the mail I received a note and a newspaper clipping from my sister back in Indiana. The clipping was from the obituary page and was about Max's funeral. Max had committed suicide. When I was a kid growing up I always thought that Max had everything going for him and I was envious of Max. I reckon that things aren't always what they appear to be.

Jimmy Boys was another good buddy of mine. He was a little on the nutty side but could always make you laugh. I remember one study hall class we had together in high school. All of the desks were lined up in rows facing the front of the class room. The teacher's desk was at the back of the class room where he could keep an eye on our activities. Jimmy was always late for study hall, so the teacher told him the next time he was late for class he would be sent to the principal's office. Sure enough, the day arrived when Jimmy was late for class again. The teacher was sitting at his desk at the back of the class room and had not yet taken attendance. All of the class room was very quiet and intent on studying, or at least making the appearance of studying. I looked over to the side entrance of the class room and there was Jimmy, squatted down in the hallway with a finger raised to his lips indicating the "quiet" signal. He pointed to the teacher's whereabouts in the class room and indicated to me that I was to let him know when the coast was clear. Now those study room desks were of the old wooden type, still mounted on the wood runners. There was one small space between the desks that Jimmy planned to utilize in order to reach his desk in the second row of desks just inside the class room. I looked back at the teacher's desk and saw that the teacher was still looking down at some paperwork and gave Jimmy the okay sign to go ahead. Jimmy took off in the fastest duck-walk I've ever seen anyone do—and he probably would have made it to his desk before the teacher would have known anything about his tardiness, except for one mistake. Just before Jimmy reached his desk in this slouched-down duck walk, he tripped over his own two feet, made one hell of a commotion, catapulted his face into the corner of the desk, and got a black eye out of the deal. He still got to see the principal anyway. Last I heard ... Jimmy was an insurance agent.

All of our days are numbered ... some more so than others. If there's a rhyme or a reason, I haven't figured it out yet. I reckon that there's some cowboy logic in there somewhere. I do know that it's better to treat others as if you might never have the opportunity to do so again, and a lot of times that's the way things turn out. Whether they are a Mr. MacInish, a Ron Hamilton, a Hershel Dunnigan, a Max Ennis or a Jimmy Boys—each unknowingly becomes an integral part of another person's life.

I still recall other stories and fond instances from those days. I gave up my share of any family inheritance a long time ago back there in southern Indiana—and rightfully so. I found that in growing up ... some things must be given up. You can't take it all with you so you have to take the most important items. Like preparing for an extended trip to a faraway land, you sift and sort through it all until you finally determine the most essential things you must have for the journey ahead, and leave the rest behind. But I'll always take with me ... the memories.

PARADISE

I woke *up* this morning, but the wind blew me *down*. It was dark when that old alarm clock started sounding off. I tried to *spring* forward but my left knee had me hobbling. I stomped that wooly spider that had bitten my knee in my sleep and went outside to do chores and to pitchfork hay to the cattle here and in Nebraska. (I figured that's where most of the hay ended up.) That terminology, *High Wind Warning* is an understatement. It should be called *Shrapnel Warning* and tell everyone to seek shelter immediately!

It's one thing to *lean* into the wind but it gets darn ridiculous when you have to turn sideways and stay at a forty-five degree angle just to stay upright, all the while dodging an assortment of flying debris that probably originated somewhere out there in California. Here in Wyoming if we didn't have the wind, we wouldn't have any weather, but at least it's warmer now. It's that time of the year when we perform the ritual stripper-act of *long johns on … long johns off.* (I must be getting older because of all of those hot-flashes I've been having lately.)

Some of the grass even has some green in it now. That's saying a lot for Wyoming. Why just a couple of days ago I was sloshing through the snow and mud. Who would have thought there was actually *terra firma* beneath all of that slop? Thanks to the wind a lot of it has dried out … including me. I like the rugged look cowboys get with wind-burned face, chaffed nose and lips, dried skin hanging off the ears and snot smeared on both cheeks. What a manly picture … the cows look better than us!

I've often wondered that if I had a choice of paradise just what the weather would be like there. I suppose it would have to be *comfortable.* Then I got to thinking what *comfortable* really is. I mean, what is comforting to me isn't necessarily comforting to other folks. What is too hot or too cold? Which is the best season? Should I be wearing clothing to be comfortable or would it be better to be streaking around instead? How about a little breeze or a touch of wind? What should paradise's elevation be? And what about the humidity level? Should there be clear skies or a few clouds throwing shadows across the landscape? What type of wildlife would be there?

That's a lot of things I'd have to consider in my choice of paradise! Guess I'll just have to settle for Wyoming instead. (At this elevation it's about as close to heaven and *paradise* that I'm going to get.) I did figure out in the process that paradise probably wouldn't be a boring place. With Wyoming weather one never needs to worry about the same old thing. So let the wind blow and I'll take the good days with the bad ones. Just be kind to this old man … and be gentle.

THANKFUL

I send many emails out to folks and I receive many emails in return. Some of those email recipients never acknowledge my emails at all. That's okay because I know how *busy* they must be. It would be difficult for me to define *busy* utilizing other folk's terminology. I'm *busy* too but I still take the time to write. The way I figure it, I'm probably busier than those who never respond at all. I reckon that if I was in a constant state of drug or alcohol-induced stupor I would be *busy* too—but I'm not. So I've decided to refine my list of certain email recipients that never respond and *tune them out*, so to speak. This will be my last email to those selected few.

Thanksgiving is just a few days away. I am thankful for so many things and I give thanks each and every night for my blessings. *Heavenly Father, please watch over Amanda and Thomas. Keep them safe from harm and in good health. Guide them in their endeavors. Forgive them of their sins, as I give thanks for the blessings they have received. Watch over their families, their friends and their loved ones. Grant them the strength, the wisdom, and the courage to do thy will. For this I ask and pray in your name. Amen.* A simple day's-end prayer that has been answered so many times.

My first horse was named *Red Wing.* She was a Quarter Horse around fifteen hands high and she came from Texas. I was about sixteen years old when I found her lying at the bottom of a ravine. I stayed with her and I carried many square bales of hay down that ravine and propped her up against the bales so that she could continue to breathe okay. When it got dark I climbed back out of that ravine and returned home, praying that she would survive the night. The next morning I climbed back down that ravine and found my *Red Wing* had died. Beside her was a still-born foal. And I cried. So many times we had run with the wind.

My second horse was named *Scout.* Not as tall as *Red Wing* but he still had a good heart and lots of stamina. (Like me, he was a bit stubborn.) He too was a Quarter Horse, but he was a palomino instead of a bay in color, as was *Red Wing.* But I loved him just the same, and then I grew apart from him when I went off to college. My father sold him when I left for the university. He later explained that there was no one to ride him or who could handle him anymore since I was gone. Then again … there was no longer anyone who could *handle* me either. (I found out when I returned from a college break that *Scout* was gone.)

I was engaged for nearly four years before I married my first wife—Nancy. We were so young and so in love. I was stupid and foolish, and yet somehow we survived a four-year marriage. It seemed the proper thing to do … to get married after so many years of engagement. (No children from that marriage.) I still broke her heart. I gave up everything I owned for my second wife—Karla, but made it through twenty-three years of marriage. I have since been blessed with two wonderful children. This time, it was the other way around … she broke my heart. There will be no *third-time charm* for this ol' boy. *You don't have to practice to be miserable.*

For all of the blessings I have received in my life—I am thankful. And for all of the misfortunes in my life—I am deserving. *What goes around comes around.* But this Thanksgiving day I am mostly thankful—thankful for the family and friends that have stayed by my side through both the good times and the rough times. And I will continue to do the same for you. And to those who neither cared nor possessed any compassion whatsoever, but always demanded something owed to them … you have heard the last from me. Cowboy Up!

PERSONAL HYGIENE

I love abusing my body. I probably have more *chemicals* in my system than Dow Chemical ever dreamt of. I counteract that with fresh air, sunshine and the wind in my hair. (Actually, I don't have too much hair atop this head of mine, but there are a multitude of *hares* in this area to compensate for that.) I keep this top-knot of mine clean cut because I've never outgrown the fear that one of these days those pesky Indians will show up at my doorstep searching for another scalp. I may disappoint them but it beats cuttin' on my noggin. My short hair is a carry-over from those old Army days. (My daughter says I have a Bruce Willis haircut.) All I know is that once I throw that old cowboy hat of mine at a bull chasing after me I can run a hell of a lot faster. (It could be the haircut or it could be the bull—*psychology* is a wonderful thing!)

They say that *cleanliness is next to godliness.* I reckon that's as close to heaven that I'm ever going to get because I take a shower every night. I know some folks who take a shower once a month—whether they need it or not. (If you stand downwind from them you can tell right away if it's towards the end of the month or not.) I get dirty every working day. (I think dirty thoughts every day—working or not.) But one thing I cannot do is to crawl into bed at the end of the day smelling like a bull's ass. So I take a shower.

A lot of folks I know take a shower the first thing in the morning. Not me—no sir! When I get up in the morning the one thought I have is getting ready for another day's work. I know it's going to be brutal, somewhat stressful and of course, dirty. I like hot showers. I want the whole damn bathroom to steam-up like a sauna. The only way I'm going to get clean after another hard day's work is to *steam-clean* me! Besides, it's good for my arthritis. At night, a hot shower with a shot of whisky and a beer and I can damn near whip the whole world—if they come at me one at a time.

Mango Peach is good smellin' stuff—that's what I use for shampoo. (I'd use it on my cow kickers but I don't think it does much good for leather.) Smells good though, and the cattle love me for using it. (It beats what they're using.) The biggest problem I have during the winter months are my fingertips cracking and bleeding. The only hand cream I've found that works relative well for me is *Aquaphor Original Ointment*—it's good for severely dry skin. I buy it at Wal-Mart for about sixteen bucks a jar. When that fails I resort to my old remedy of super glue. A little dab of that stuff on my fingertips and the healing process begins. It stings a bit when I squirt it on my fingers but it's better than that spray-on bandage crap that washes off anyway. I'll say one thing about super glue—it doesn't wash off! (You just gotta' be careful where you put it.)

Personal hygiene is important to me. A clean bandanna is just as important as clean underwear. My mother used to say; "*Ronnie, always make sure you wear clean underwear—that way if you end up in the hospital you won't be embarrassed.*" The way I figured it was that if I did end up in the hospital the last thing I was going to worry about was my underwear—but I took her advice. I always figured that if you were in an accident your underwear would tell the whole story anyway. You gotta' love you mom for caring about you though.

I try to shave once a day—usually at night. The cows don't really care what I look like in the morning but my pillowcase sure appreciates it when I go to sleep. I've been known to *sand* a few fair maiden's hide during the daylight hours, but never at nighttime. Yep, I'm a *real diamond in the rough*! Oh yea, if I want to smell a little bit on the tangy side I just apply some *Old Spice* aftershave. So some day if you look out across the prairie and see a whole herd of heifers chasing some old cowpoke—it's just me, running for my life!

PISS ANT DRUGGIE

Back when I was a *Piss Ant* I believed myself to be invincible. Nowadays, with all of those commercials on television I realize how vulnerable I am to a multitude of ailments that could possibly afflict me at any time. How I ever survived this long without those advertised medical remedies is beyond my comprehension. I don't watch television too often because there's usually nothing on that's worth watching, but when I do tune-in I am bombarded with ads on how to improve my health. I recently read that the largest group of drug users today was the *Baby-Boomer* generation—surpassing even the young adults in their late teens and early twenties. Duh—well hell yes, we were raised on drugs. You think we're going to give them up in our older age? Not!

The older we get the more we need our drugs. We need to have something to break up that high cholesterol. A little pain reliever for that arthritis. An aspirin a day to keep the heart pumping. (Like a Timex—it takes a lickin' but keeps on tickin'.) Oh yea—don't forget those other "extremities" for the men out there. Got to get that old flag pole up there. Women don't want to loose too much calcium because they won't be able to "support" others. If you've got a headache you can now just "rub" it away. (I just wish I could rub some things away.) Women can color their hair to look younger and men can now grow a new bush on their head. We can now get rid of the puggies by ordering special food without even working out. *They're Kate's eyes but they're my responsibility*—so says Pearle Vision. (I've got news for you Buster—they're my eyes and they're <u>my</u> responsibility!)

What a comfortable feeling to be in the thoughts of so many concerned medical authorities. Restless Leg Syndrome (RLS) is the newest ailment—that's when your legs start doing funny things while you're lying back in your recliner chair watching the boob tube. It's a good thing I don't have a recliner chair or I could develop RLS. They've got a drug for that too. (My solution is to put that bag of chips down and get your fat ass out of that chair and move around! No drugs required.)

I know that some drugs serve a purpose. Like marijuana for example—it helps ease the pain, the eyesight ... or hindsight. It helps something—I think I remember though I'm not really sure ... Alcohol is still the number one selling drug and I aim to keep it right up there at the top of the list. (A powerful thirst is a horrible thing to endure.) If all else fails you can always elect to have surgery—please see your doctor first. It never hurts to have a second opinion. If you're going to work on yourself start with a small section first ... just like using a fabric cleaner. You want to make sure that you don't botch the larger area. No—I haven't seen that as a commercial yet ... but I know it's coming.

I use Aleve for my arthritis, aspirin for colds and whisky for generalized aches and pains. I've known many living examples of folks who were suffering from one ailment or another and yet survived through sheer self-determination ... without the use of drugs of any kind. (Perhaps they didn't have television and they didn't know any better.) For some things there are no remedies—for everything else … there's Master Card. One of the strongest examples of self-determination was a man I met many years ago. He endured to the very end when he suffered a terrible accident while at work. His head was cut off and yet … he never said a word!

THAT OLD MAN

I first met the old man years ago—he taught me a lot. The man that I knew then has long since gone but not the lessons he generously bestowed upon me. He was a mixture of *roughness* and *sternness*, with *wisdom, compassion* and *patience* for an upstart hard-headed guy such as me. (At times he really pissed me off!) But somewhere along the way his lessons took a hold of me, though I didn't understand it at the time, and I wouldn't realize what actually *sunk in* until years later. It's funny how things mean so little when you're young and immortal.

He taught me to take three shallow breaths and hold the last one, then gently pull the trigger with the tip of my forefinger—don't *squeeze* that trigger! He taught me that in the darkness of night one can see better using peripheral vision than looking directly at something. Study your surroundings and be aware of everything about you. Above all, remember that *movement* is what gets you killed, or allows you to kill what you failed to see previously. Remember … you *always* hit where you're aiming!

The old man cautioned me not to speak so freely and to keep others guessing—better for them to think they know the *real you* than to give them a complete biography that they can use against you later. He taught me when you have that feeling of *fire in the gut* that it was an indication of what *freedom* was—a feeling he further explained that most people neither had nor would risk their life for. *Tough love*, he explained, was better than no love at all and that most people couldn't comprehend the difference between love and a convenience for their present situation. He told me it was better to forsake your present situation than to continue to live life as a living hell.

The old man said to cherish true friendship. He further explained that a friend that throws you away after one situation wasn't a *friend* to begin with. Beware of those who tell stories about you—true or not, they have their own agenda. Watch out for those particular individuals such as the farmer who was *outstanding in his field* or the person who was a *legend in his own mind*. (The old man had a way with words.) "Humor" he said, made life tolerable and that Cowboys were closer to the likes of angels than most folks realized—except when they were inebriated (both angels and cowboys).

Experience would always replace book-learning. *Trial and error* was better than not trying at all. He said that a good horse was like a good woman and that when you got bucked off you had get back on again. (I think the old man had something else on his mind.) He told me that if you'd never been "touched" by a raging bull and lived through it then you've never appreciated *life*. He also said that there was a *fine line* between life and death and that if you didn't know what side you were walking on then you were probably dead—or should have been. He also showed me that the *business-end* of a rope was not the end around an ornery steer's horns—but that end of the rope where your saddle horn was. The old man told me to never throw a loop at something I couldn't hold on to. (I guess I never really learned that one because I'll still throw *loops* at things I can't hold on to.)

I became *rich* so many years ago that today's multi-millionaire looks like a pauper compared to me. I don't expound upon my financial portfolio and that I'd never have to work another day in my life if I chose to do so. Yeah, that's right—rich, rich, filthy rich. But I wouldn't trade the life I live for some cheap multimillion condominium in Manhattan for anyone. Take me for whom I am. I'm just a guy that *Old Man* took some time-out for to teach me some lessons … oh so many years ago. The old man, he taught me well.

GONE ARE THE DAYS

Gone are the days of freedom in the West. Nowadays everyone is accountable to society at large, or so they tell us. For instance, the wannabe "metropolitan" city of Cheyenne enacted a smoking ban for all of the restaurants and bars in town. (I reckon the citizens of Wyoming are becoming more like their liberal counterparts in Colorado who long ago relinquished their individualism.) I'm not saying that smoking is healthy for anyone. Secondhand smoke is just as deadly for nonsmokers. But now there is no choice. If you were a waitress working in a smoking establishment you once had a choice of waiting tables or quitting. Now you get to work in a smoke-free environment. To hell with the smoking customer and likewise … to hell with business profits. If you think for one moment I'm going outside in twenty-degree weather and a forty mile an hour wind to smoke a cigarette you've got another thought coming. No sir! I'll tell you what I will do though. I'll make sure I empty out the cigarette butts in my truck's ashtray on the streets of Cheyenne before I head back to the ranch.

You used to be able to get "loaded" in an out-of-town local bar and drive the old gravel roads back to the ranch without worrying about the Fuzz pulling you over for being intoxicated. The worst that could happen was that you could run off the road and end up in some barrow ditch. Nowadays, Barney Fife wants to give you a DUI and a court appearance. You know what I like about law-enforcement these days? Yep, you guessed it—not a damn thing! The deputy dogs should remain in town taking care of all those sewer rats and the crime-infested population of Cheyenne and leave the poor cowhand alone. I'm being fair here you know—I'll drink my whisky and you can eat your doughnuts. The way I figure it, if you can't take care of yourself then you are a detriment to society and one step away from welfare.

Oh I know … we need laws to "govern" society. Otherwise, only the strongest would survive. What a horrible thought—survival of the fittest! That's almost like *Nature* … and we all know how screwed-up *Nature* is. Makes me wonder why all of those millions of tourists flock to the national parks and wilderness areas in the summertime then beat-feet home before it gets too cold and winter sets in. Come to think of it, I don't see too many RV's around here anymore. (Might have something to do with our first snow of the season here on the on the 23rd of this month.) It's okay if you don't want to experience the life I live through all seasons of the year. But then, don't tell me how I should live my life. I don't have the choice of running to a warm shelter when the weather changes for the worse. Neither do the cattle. Reckon that's why they call us *Cowhands*.

I could never be a banker living on the money of others. What a detestable existence screwing-over others. Feeling all powerful while feeding off the misery of the less-privileged. A bad day for a banker is a paper cut. A bad day for the cowhand is not getting paid the month's wages owed to him—on time. (Makes him wonder what all of that work was for.) A good day for a banker is approving a loan for someone who really doesn't need one. A good day for a cowhand is sharing a meal with another cowhand who is less fortunate than himself. Yea—go ahead and tell me I'm full of crap with my comparisons. Then search you heart and tell me I'm wrong.

Nobody in their right mind would want to be a poor busted-up cowhand. Who in the hell wants to work for someone who owns everything—even your own time and wages? Agriculture is one of the most dangerous occupations in the United States. Small agricultural businesses such as ranching elude many of the mandatory governmental work standards. The individuals that work in this type of environment are either tramps or professionals. The tramps don't last too long because they're usually looking for a place to lay low or to dry out for awhile until they can collect enough wages to move on to better pastures. But the real cow-hand does what he does all for the love of the life he lives and his "better pasture" is the one he's standing in. If I have to explain this to you then your elevator is stuck between floors. For some, I could write it all down on a good piece of two-by-four and smack them up the side of the head and they still wouldn't get it.

Gone are the days when an individual's path in life could mean real freedom. Today, everyone belongs to someone and everything belongs to something. We teach math and science in our schools but ignore *individual art*. No wonder we produce so many educated morons. (If we can't watch it on television, touch it or see it—then we no longer believe it exists.) To *dream* is to believe that anything is possible. Gone are the days of individual sustainability—to work with one's own hands and mind and to see their efforts blossom. We have become what others would wish of us. You cannot "teach" art. Gone are the days of throwing an empty beer can out the truck window without someone reporting the litter viola-tion or a DUI on their cell phone. Gone are the days of *out of sight, out of mind*. Now, we must conform, think and believe like everyone else. I believe in myself and I believe that … *gone are the days*.

PRIDE IN FREEDOM

I couldn't imagine a life without *freedom*, or living without *pride*. I'm stubborn, that's indisputable—but I still retain a conscience and a real *caring* for others, regardless what others may think of me. One of my many failings is that I don't always display my feelings to other folks. Then again sometimes, I do when I'm not in the best of moods, and I wish I'd kept my mouth shut! It takes me awhile to *blow-up* but when I do, Katie bar the door! (Anyone is a fair target then.)

I plan to publish my next book in 2007. It'll probably get me in more trouble than I'm in presently, but that's okay. (Hell, if I wasn't in trouble half of the time I wouldn't feel normal anyway.) I won't expound too much about what my next book is about except that it will be more *local* in nature and I'll be writing about real folks I've come to know and respect in Wyoming. Most of the manuscript is completed but I still have loose ends to tie up. (I'll have this winter to begin wrapping things up.) If you don't care about cowhands, ranchers and their fami-lies or the fast disappearing rural aspects of Wyoming then you probably won't want to read it. Enough said on the subject.

We are quickly losing our western heritage—and with that go *freedom* and *pride*. Today's world is nothing akin to the 1800's and the early 1900's here in

Wyoming. There are too many housing additions with forty-acre lots with land-owners believing themselves to be *ranchers,* littering once good grazing land where the only night sound under heavenly skies was an occasional bawl from the old *boss* calling for her calf. (That folks is real testimony of a good mother!) The *Old-Timers* I've known and respected for so many years now are dwindling in numbers. It will be a sorry day when they're gone!

I couldn't imagine a life without a beat-up cowboy hat, bandanna, cow-kicking boots, chaps and cow manure speckling my face. I realize that doesn't sound romantic to most people. As a young farm boy back in southern Indiana in early 1968, I read an article in the *National Geographic Magazine* about Wyoming (accompanied with black and white photos) depicting the real West. I wrote a letter to the Cheyenne Chamber of Commerce requesting help in finding me a job working on a ranch in Wyoming. I received a letter from the Cattail Ranch. The day following my high school graduation I was on a Greyhound bus from Indianapolis to Cheyenne with a one-way bus ticket costing me $35.40. What little money I had left in my billfold I guarded with my life! (Thirty-eight years later my total savings is still somewhere around thirty-five dollars and forty cents…. so I haven't lost anything in the process.)

What I have lost is a sense of freedom—but not my pride. That's why when I go to town I still wear my cowboy hat and boots. I may look out of place compared to today's *urban cowboy* but I really don't give a damn what others think. Most of the time when I'm in town the folks I chat with are appreciative and courteous towards me, and I return their graciousness. Then there are others who view me from another planet. I'm not particularly fond of the term of *Cowboy.* I prefer the word *Cowhand.* After all, that's what I am—a *hand* who takes care of cows. And I still ride for the brand.

When you give up your heritage you surrender your soul. The problem is that it's usually too late when you realize that it's all gone forever. I once told Jay Berry that when I couldn't take a piss out on the prairie without someone seeing me then it was time to move on. It's a good thing I did—now there are forty-acre lots near where I once thought that privacy prevailed. If I knew then what I know now, I would have crossed that road and took care of my business on the other side of the fence.

AUTUMN

Autumn. Yellow gold with a splash of red and frost on the morning windshield. Long johns with early light and finding a place to hang them by midmorning. Snow on far mountain peaks and a gentler but biting wind. Pronghorn bucks establishing their territory with waves of antelope herds traveling up and over the distant hills. When it is overcast now it is colder and there is more darkness than there is light in a typical day. I run into some folks I know and they ask me how's it going? I say, *Good … since I gave up hope.* But autumn … autumn always seems to lift my spirits.

Perhaps it's the end of a cycle or the beginning of a new one—I really can't say for sure. I just know it's what turns my crank. October is my favorite time of the year here in Wyoming. It adds another year to my life and the belief that "wisdom" can't be too far behind. I do a lot of *venting* in my emails and say a lot of things that some folks question me about. When I further explain my intentions they sometimes understand me better … then sometimes not. It's easier to make up a story than to tell a lie. After all, stories are more plausible.

I've had a lot of stories told about me—or maybe they were just lies. Some were half-truths and then some were really real. I've found that given enough time if someone keeps telling the same story about you that eventually it becomes the truth. I reckon I'm the only one that knows for sure. My memory is pretty good. I remember things that other folks never heard of—maybe it never really happened, but I still remember it anyway. My philosophy has always been to tell others what you want them to hear. Then (if they're really listening) they just might possibly understand the thoughts behind the spoken words.

Autumn is like that for me … what you see and feel is not what it seems. Autumn wears a mask as a disguise. All that color gives comfort to one's soul and marks a time for inner reflection. But it is a *lie* in the broadest of terms. Fall seduces. It is a half-truth of what is to come. It is beautiful and mankind is susceptible to beauty. I for one see beauty where others see only the person. Wrinkles tell a loving story as graying hair betrays understanding. But it is the individual's eyes that tell the real story. When I look into another person's eyes as they are speaking to me I come to an understanding of what that particular individual is about. I can tell in an instant whether it is a lie, just a conversation to pass the time, or a genuine interest between the two of us. And sometimes … just sometimes—it is more than all of that.

A dear friend of mine recently wrote me asking if I had any success in *finding a cowgirl.* I replied there was *No cowgirl in my life. I don't actively pursue finding someone—which would account for their absence. I would sure like to find that spe-cial someone but I don't think that will happen.* My friend's reply: *Can you tell me why you would not try?* I answered: *I have nothing to offer.* The way I figure it … love is a bartering system of the oldest kind. I'm just too tired to barter—I'm at the age where I want it all or nothing. So, as usually happens … I settle for nothing.

Autumn begins hunting season—*blood on the moon.* The sight of blood doesn't bother me because to me … blood is life. Stem the flow and breathe the musky air. Rattle the antlers and follow the track. Gently kiss a cold neck while covering the warmth of another's body with your own. There's always another round in the chamber. There's always another tomorrow. There's always another season. But autumn … autumn is mine!

I STILL BELIEVE

I still believe. I believe that for every cold and bitter winter day there's a warm one on the way—it's just hard to imagine. I believe that *Old Grand Dad* 100% proof Kentucky straight bourbon whisky has saved my life more than once. I know that you can't blow a frozen nose until it thaws and that it is not wise to wipe the ice cycles off your moustache until you warm up. I believe the best sex is unplanned (it just happens). I also know that the yearling heifer I just chased all over the pasture isn't really that stupid—like all women she's just playing games with me, and I do love it so.

I still believe, if you have the time, that a good horse surpasses all other forms of transportation. I also know that anyone who rides bulls is a bit touched in the head and has more macho than brains. I believe that anything mechanical can be fixed—and I've proven that fact countless times, while lessening my wallet. I know that money doesn't buy everything but it comes damn close in doing so. I also believe in free enterprise as long as I'm the beneficiary.

I believe that *giving* is better than *receiving.* I believe in Saint Nicholas and the spirit of Christmas but I'm not too sure about Santa Claus. (I've always wondered how a fat ass in a red suit can get down the chimney.) I believe that antelope can still run at thirty-five mph though I haven't "clocked" them with that old truck for awhile. I know that from a distance, sheep out on the prairie still look like range maggots and that Hollywood's attempt with the movie *Brokeback Mountain* was nothing more than another gimmick to demeanor the cowboy culture of the American west.

I believe that good women, like a good men, are scarce—that the best one can do is to settle for the best in someone else and pray that they don't uncover too many faults in you. I believe that an unloaded gun is just about as useful as a hammer—and that you might as well throw an unloaded gun at your attacker as you would throw a hammer. I believe in life after death ... but with a loaded gun I believe I'll arrive there later than most folks. (I know that you can never have too much ammunition.)

I believe that the older one gets the more likely the hair on top your head moves southward ... seeking warmer climates (that's plain human nature). I know that the handsomer you were in youth the more likely you are to age as good wine—and if you were ugly when young you haven't a ghost's chance in hell of making it when you get older. I believe in genetics and ... *Maboline*. I believe that every good deed deserves another in return.

I believe that when I finally die I want to do so in *peace*. I know I want to be remembered as one who tried to do what was right and honorable and who cared about others. I believe the greatest reward is to be remembered as a *brother* of mankind, and pray that in the end my attributes will outweigh my deficiencies. I know the fear of loneliness far more so than I know the comforting feeling of companionship, but strive to overcome the former through the help of others.

I believe that a good kick in the pants is better than getting too serious about oneself. I know that there is a cure for every illness, if only in another's embrace or a simple handshake. I know that *humor* "heals" ... at least momentarily. I believe that a shit-eatin' smile is better than no smile at all. I relish the flicker of another person's eyes that betrays their life. I know that I'll never be perfect but that I'll eventually become damn close to it because ... *I believe*!

CHASING DREAMS

This has been a trilogy of work experiences working as a cowhand with the Cattail Ranch, Berry's Herefords and the R Bar H Ranch. I wish to personally thank Rod Kirkbride, Jay Berry and Norman "Buck" Holmes for allowing me the time and the giving of their patience, so that I might work and provide my perspectives. I know that what I have written in these pages may not *sit* well with these three Wyoming ranchers in every instance, but nonetheless, I respect each of them. If I have made errors in judgment, the English language, or depicted individuals in an unfair manner—then these mistakes are mine alone. I wrote each *essay* at the time the event took place, as such, that certain objectiveness could not be obtained at the time of writing.

My writings would never have been possible without the support and more importantly, the *understanding*, of a very special person that entered my life several years ago. And though our *companionship* has since been terminated, the fond memories of Michel Paxson and her supportiveness in my effort to place thoughts into written form will never be forgotten. Michel was my *kick in the pants* to get me moving and I did just that, unfortunately … I kept moving further and further away and did what I consider the most reprehensible act of all—I broke a sacred trust between us and my own heart in the process. She understood me better than I understood myself at the time. Thank you Michel, for having the guts and determination to place your faith in a losing proposition such as myself. Your *love* and understanding will always be remembered by this old cowhand.

It has been said that we are a *product* of our environment. Should that be the case, and I believe it to be so, then perhaps I am no worse off than those with whom I associate. This cowhand's perspective may not be *relative* in all instances—after all, it is only one man's opinion and opinions are like, well … we all have one. I know that I cannot continue this life such as I have lived it these past few years. Age has a way of catching up with everyone and so it is with me as well. It's only a matter of time when I must decide to hang up my spurs for the last time. For me there has always been a moment of reminisce when I loosen the cinch and remove my saddle from a horse's sweaty back at the end of the day. We both made it—both horse and man, safely without injury to the other while accomplishing the task at hand.

My hope is that, you the reader, made it through this book safely and without too much injury to yourself. I have not always been a *polite* host and oftentimes I have turned away those I admire and care about the most. I am at times abrupt, arrogant, opinionated, brash and hard headed—just a few characteristics of an otherwise perfectly normal human being. But it is you, the reader, who is my audience and the substance of this man's life—my *horse*, whom I never would have accomplished the task at hand if it were not for you.

So the work is done. My horse has been cooled off and groomed and is now ready to be returned to the open range. The saddle and tack have been hung, the light turned off and the door to the barn closed for another day. I turn towards the direction of home then pause for a moment, and watch as my horse rolls back and forth on his back in the dust, gets up and shakes himself off. I have the feeling that perhaps you'll want to do the same sort of thing. Thank you for *Coming In* …

978-0-595-42486-3
0-595-42486-4